Left Coast
Roast

HANNA
NEUSCHWANDER

Left Coast Roast

Portland · **TIMBER PRESS** · London

A GUIDE TO THE BEST COFFEE
AND ROASTERS FROM
SAN FRANCISCO TO SEATTLE

COPYRIGHT © 2012
BY HANNA NEUSCHWANDER.
ALL RIGHTS RESERVED.

DESIGN BY BREANNA GOODROW
ILLUSTRATIONS BY ALLISON BERG & RYAN BUSH

PUBLISHED IN 2012
BY TIMBER PRESS, INC.

THE HASELTINE BUILDING
133 S.W. SECOND AVE., SUITE 450
PORTLAND, OREGON 97204-3527
TIMBERPRESS.COM

2 THE QUADRANT
135 SALUSBURY ROAD
LONDON NW6 6RJ
TIMBERPRESS.CO.UK

PRINTED IN
THE U.S.A.

Library of Congress Cataloging-in-Publication Data
Neuschwander, Hanna.
        Left Coast Roast : A Guide to the Best Coffee and Roasters
from San Francisco to Seattle / Hanna Neuschwander. -- First [edition].
                pages cm
        Includes bibliographical references and index.
        ISBN 978-1-60469-284-6
 1. Coffee. 2. Coffee--processing. 3. Coffee brewing. 4. Coffee
industry--Pacific States. I. Title.
        TX415.N48 2012
        641.3'373--Dc23
                                        2011050644

TO GREYSTON

AND ESMÉ

AND ALL

THE OTHER

FUTURE

COFFEE

DRINKERS

OF AMERICA

Contents

COFFEE PRIMER

22

ACKNOWLEDGMENTS

The people and companies profiled in this book gave much more freely of their time and knowledge than I had any right to expect, teaching me every step of the way. Coffee is complicated; in order to try to simplify it in my own mind, I turned countless times to the writings of Tom Own and Maria Troy (of sweetmarias.com) as well as to the older but still exhaustive writings of Kenneth Davids. Anyone with an interest in coffee would do well to start with the treasure trove of information penned by these individuals.

I am deeply grateful for the people who taught me to love coffee in the first place, especially Chris and Celeste Brady, and for the friendship of many wonderful baristas and roasters. For their insights and feedback, I thank Adrian Hale, Hannah Wallace, Anna Wolk, Justin Johnson, Paul Thornton, Jared Linzmeier, Oliver Stormshak, Andrew Barnett, Mark Hellweg, Connie Blumhardt, and Marcus Young. For helping me understand that writing about coffee is nearly as much fun as drinking it, thanks to Ben Waterhouse, Kelly Clarke, and Sarah Allen. For his patience and advice, John gets a thousand gold stars. And to Mom and Pete: your love is an inexhaustible source of strength. Thanks also to this book's editors for their guidance, Juree Sondker, Mindy Fitch, and Eve Goodman.

Preface

IN ONE OF the last conversations between coffee kingpin Alfred Peet and his master roaster John Weaver, Peet said he wished to see more small coffee companies "sprinkled throughout the land" in place of the "big corporate leviathans lumbering about."

Peet passed away in 2007, but in many ways his vision is just coming to fruition. In the pages of this book, you will find profiles of dozens of those smaller roasting companies, many of which have opened shop since 2005. But you will also find profiles of some of the leviathans responsible for building coffee culture as we know it on the West Coast and across the U.S., and without whom small roasters wouldn't exist.

For me, coffee is two wonderful things: a social ritual and an aesthetic experience. As I learn more about coffee and the people who produce it, I find the ritual becoming richer and every cup somehow tasting better. Knowledge is a vivid sweetener. I hope that in the course of reading this book you discover a little something that sweetens your cup. I also hope you find yourself inspired to dig in on your own—learn the name of the barista or coffee roaster who makes your favorite cappuccino, try something you've never tried, take the time to make your own coffee on a Sunday morning, or roast your own on a Saturday afternoon.

This book celebrates the incredible variety of options available to coffee lovers on the West Coast, but of course it can only scratch the surface. The fifty-five roasters profiled here are but a small fraction of the action taking place—at least fifty coffee roasters reside in Portland, Oregon, alone, where I live. I selected these particular roasters for many reasons—because they are iconic, historic, unusual, exceptional, cutting edge, or in some cases because I felt personally drawn to their approach. I also considered the individual story of each roaster. Collectively these profiles tell a larger story about West Coast coffee culture and its evolution since the 1960s.

HOW TO USE THIS BOOK

The introduction and Coffee Primer examine changes in the coffee world and provide some basic information on what coffee roasting is (and how to roast your own), where coffee comes from, and how to make a decent cup at home. Other useful information, like where the flavors in coffee come from and how to keep track of when coffee is in season, is sprinkled throughout.

The meat of the book—profiles of coffee roasters in California, Oregon, and Washington—can be used however suits you best: as a guidebook, travel guide, or catalog for online shopping needs.

Favorite

My own favorite roasters are indicated with a star. They are favorites for various reasons, but they generally share a passion for the seemingly endless variety and nuance of coffee, and this passion infuses every aspect of their work. From thoughtfully designed cafés, to information-packed websites, to careful preparation, these roasters are committed to beautiful coffee and the stories behind it.

WHERE TO GET THE COFFEE

Each roaster profile lists the most noteworthy locations at which you can find the coffee (for example, the roastery, original café, or flagship café) and provides information about whether the roaster operates other cafés or offers coffee online. Most roasters also supply their coffee to some combination of local grocery stores, independent cafés, or restaurants, though such wholesale accounts are too numerous and changeable to list.

If you are able to visit a café operated by the roaster, you will be treated to a remarkable experience. Roasters who have taken such care to find the best beans and roast them to their peak potential don't generally drop the ball by ruining the coffee at the counter. So, if you can, visit a roaster-operated café.

Short of that, buying coffee online is easier than ever, and the cost of shipping is made up for by guaranteed freshness. All but a handful of the roasters profiled in this book offer their beans online. Those that don't, make coffee too tasty to exclude, even though you have to show up in person for a cup. Many roasters also feature clubs or subscription services, which provide you with your favorite coffee—or send something new and different—on a regular schedule. A few websites also offer subscriptions combining coffees from different roasters. Check out Citizen Bean (citizenbean.com), Craft Coffee (craftcoffee.com), and Go Coffee Go (gocoffeego.com).

CAVEATS

Coffee changes all the time. The availability of it changes as seasons, governments, weather, shipping companies, and economies allow. Growing, harvesting, and processing methods change and evolve. New farmers come along. None of the coffees described in this book will be available forever, and flavors change from roast to roast. But imagine buying the same bottle of wine every time. Comfort and habit are great, but coffee is better—try something new. Roasters' websites are the best source for up-to-date information.

THE

Quality

REVOLUTION

SO FAR it's been a good millennium for coffee lovers. In contrast, through most of the twentieth century, Americans were happy to drink cheap, low-quality or instant coffee. It was something you made at home (or drank at Denny's), it came preground in a can, and it preferably didn't cost more than a dollar a pound.

In the late 1960s and early 1970s, however, a cadre of coffee roasters in California, Oregon, and Washington began to reconsider the taste of coffee, led by the likes of Alfred Peet of Peet's Coffee & Tea. Over the next two decades, entrepreneurs like Howard Schultz of Starbucks took a burgeoning small movement to roast better coffees and supersized it. Through the 1990s, Starbucks opened on average one store every day around the world and convinced millions to indulge in triple grande vanilla half-caf nonfat lattes in place of the traditional cup of scorched black coffee. The hot milkshake was born. Coffee had moved out of the kitchen and into public life in a very big way.

Peet's and myriad other roasters of the time inspired a generation of people to love coffee with a new passion. Nowhere was the mantle taken up more fervently than where the movement began: on the West Coast. Since the 1990s, but especially since 2000, coffee lovers and tinkerers in California, Oregon, and Washington have worked to improve on the legacies of Peet's and Starbucks. Companies like Stumptown Coffee Roasters in Portland have contributed to a rejiggering of the coffee business on a scale both global and local. And it all lines up to a simple fact: many of the coffees described in this book are better—more nuanced in flavor, more lovingly roasted and prepared—than any coffees that have ever been available anywhere in the world. Ever.

The quality revolution's foot soldiers are a motley crew. A surprising number of roasters come from the worlds of art, food, wine, and music and regard coffee with rapturous fascination. Others are gearheads, former data analysts, engineers, or IT workers with a bias toward testing, tinkering, and open information systems. Many roasters are also relatively inexperienced, a fact that has led to some grand experiments and some equally grand failures. This book is proof of the sum total of their successes, a catalog of the wild profusion of excitement about coffee.

I call it a revolution because the changes are systemic, having rippled through the entire coffee chain. Roasters, importers, and agronomists are working directly with farmers to separate out the highest-quality beans, to improve the quality and environmental footprint of farming and processing methods, and to mitigate harmful logistical issues (for instance, storing and transporting green coffee thoughtfully). Roasters are paying more attention to how they roast coffees, and many passionate baristas are finding ways to make coffee their lifelong career.

The increasing seriousness with which coffee is treated is part of a much bigger shift in attitudes. We have entered an era in which small things done well have great value, an era that demands transparency and connectedness to story. Contemporary coffee roasters give us these things and more. Increasingly, roasters maintain blogs where they can explain where their coffees come from, post photos and videos of trips to farms, and describe the process of developing a new blend. Websites and even coffee bags provide traceability information about the farm where the beans were grown, what varietal they are, how they were processed, even when they were harvested.

Although Chicago, New York, Denver, Milwaukee, Minneapolis, and even Dallas now teem with coffee geeks, the revolution has achieved a unique momentum on the West Coast. Innovators in Oregon, Washington, and California have changed the way we understand and enjoy what's in the cup. In Portland, the number of independent coffee roasters has been increasing since the late

1990s, in a market everyone thought was already saturated. Two other hubs of coffee culture, Seattle and San Francisco, burst with energy and history. The Bay Area is among the largest and oldest ports for coffee importation in the country. A handful of roasting companies there have been in business since the 1800s, foils to a crop of new, quality-focused roasteries taking the region by storm. Seattle is a city of deep loyalties to well-established brands, but innovators are quietly making change there as well. The revolution isn't restricted to big cities, either. Quality coffee has seeped out to the margins, from Bellingham, Washington, to Fort Bragg, California. Some of the roasters profiled here are at the leading edge of these changes, while others have contentedly staked out territory somewhere along the trajectory of change. A few have remained doggedly the same as they always were, but because of deep history and past innovation have had an outsized impact on West Coast coffee.

Where to begin? Well, that's what this book is for.

glee
PRIMER

In chemical terms, coffee is among the most complex foods known to science, with more than a thousand identified flavor compounds and no single flavor fingerprint. (Compare that to fewer than thirty flavor compounds in bananas, with one compound, 3-methylbutyl acetate, contributing what we know as banana flavor.) Coffee is extremely diverse in character thanks to the thousands of varietals of *Coffea arabica* (many of them still undiscovered and unclassified), nuanced differences in how countries and regions process it, and the endless variations in how it is prepared.

This primer aims to deepen your appreciation of the coffees and coffee roasters profiled in this book—exploring, for example, why coffee tastes so mysteriously good, what seasonality means for coffee lovers, and how to try

your hand at roasting your own.
I hope this introduction will expand your enjoyment of coffee, "the king of all perfumes." Happy drinking.

THE

Lingo

TALKING about coffee, like talking about any specialized topic—wine, Dungeons & Dragons, lichen formations—involves some jargon. Some of it is usefully specific, some is helpful and fun, and some involves a bit of smoke and mirrors. Here's a quick and dirty guide to the essential lingo.

BRIGHT

When people talk about coffee being bright, they are talking about its acidity, the zinginess of it. Acids present in coffee beans imbue lively flavors—citric acid, for example, can lend a taste of tangerine or lime. Without acidity, coffee is bland and limp. Bright coffees often have exciting and complex flavors, such as the sweet pucker of Meyer lemon bracing against chocolate. But brightness can go too far, especially if a naturally bright coffee is underroasted, causing it to taste sour.

COFFEE BEANS AND COFFEE CHERRIES

Coffee beans are the seeds of the coffee cherry, which is a fruit. Coffee cherries are shaped a bit like olives but are botanically similar to pit fruits like nectarines, mangos, and yes, cherries. Coffee cherries can be either red or yellow when ripe.

CUPPING

Cupping is a formal approach to tasting coffee, usually with the purpose of evaluating its quality for export, with special attention paid to physical and taste defects. Roasters cup coffee to decide which coffees to buy and for quality control after they have purchased a coffee and are roasting it for sale. Cuppings have become popular in many upscale cafés as an approximation of wine or beer tastings. They involve loudly slurping different coffees side by side from shared cups using a deep spoon. Each coffee is tasted multiple times as it cools, revealing nuances of flavor.

DIRECT TRADE

Direct trade is a core purchasing principle for many coffee roasters focused on quality, but it is also used in marketing roasted coffee, so its meaning can seem somewhat murky at times. Early on, some roasters used the phrase to define their departure from buying Fair Trade coffees; it meant they had paid a premium beyond the Fair Trade price in order to give an incentive to coffee growers to produce better-quality coffees (quality is something Fair Trade did not historically address). Early users of the term believed face-to-face interaction was necessary and began traveling regularly to farms (hence the related phrase *relationship coffee*). Today *direct trade* generally refers to coffee whose price was directly negotiated with the farmer for the quality supplied. It rarely means that a roaster actually purchased the coffee directly from a farmer. Importers and exporters perform important roles in moving coffee around the globe, and coffee is usually purchased through these intermediaries for good reasons.

ESTATE COFFEE

Traditionally, estate coffee was defined as coffee processed in the same location where it was grown. Because so few coffee farms now have their own mills, the term has come to describe coffees from a single farm that were processed together and kept separate from other farms' coffees. (The alternative to an estate might be a cooperative—individuals farm a small plot of land and deliver their coffee to a common processing facility, where the beans are generally mixed together with other farmers' beans.) Because there are no legal restrictions on how the term is used, it's hard to know

Etiquette at the cupping table involves slurping loudly and talking softly or not at all.

whether beans labeled as estate coffee really fit the criteria unless you ask good questions of your roaster.

ETHICAL COFFEE

Consumers don't have direct knowledge of whether coffee is grown sustainably or workers are treated well, and most farmers really have no idea how much the average American pays for a quadruple latte made with their coffee beans. Many organizations and systems exist to try to ensure that people act responsibly in this inherently unequal system. But ethical coffee is complex, with no certain answers and many trade-offs. Coffees certified by various organizations (Fair Trade USA, for example) are sold for a premium; the additional money goes either to farmers or to programs aimed at improving sustainability or farmer quality of life.

Organic

For a coffee to be labeled organic, both the farm and the roasting facility must be certified, the first by a third-party certification agency and the second by the USDA. The certification process is expensive for both farmers and roasters, and fairness advocates argue that it's prohibitive for small farmers to become certified. Many very small farms operate with organic methods out of necessity—fertilizers are too expensive. Needless to say, these farms generally cannot afford organic certification. While some roasters believe that organically grown coffees can't achieve the highest levels of quality, roasters like Noble Coffee in Ashland, Oregon, are actively challenging this notion. Disheartening stories have surfaced about farmers in some countries (notably Peru) clear-cutting land to establish new organic farms, but generally organic farmers take great care with their land and tree husbandry, so you can expect an overall high level of quality. Nearly all organically grown coffee is considered specialty-grade (that is, scores 80 points or more on a 100-point scale).

Fair Trade

The Fair Trade system provides an infrastructure for small farmers to bring their coffees to a central location for milling and then sell it to buyers for a premium. The co-ops keep a portion of the premium for reinvestment in the processing infrastructure and in community projects. Fair Trade guarantees that farmers will not earn the bottom-scraping prices that keep them in dire poverty. In an effort to reinvigorate the Fair Trade model and extend its impact, in 2011 Fair Trade USA rewrote many of its rules for coffee. Most notably, the new rules allow farmers who are not part of a cooperative to participate. It's still quite early to tell what impacts these changes will have.

Shade-grown, Bird Friendly, Rainforest Alliance

Shade-grown coffee is grown under the cover of trees instead of in the open sun, which preserves biodiversity, controls erosion, protects native bird species, and often leads to better-quality coffee. Since the term can be used without restriction, look for the logo of a specific shade certification agency. Bird Friendly coffee is certified by the Smithsonian Migratory Bird Center and must meet organic standards plus a minimum of 40 percent shade coverage. Rainforest Alliance coffee is certified based on both environmental and labor-rights standards, including shade cover requirements, bans on changing natural waterways and dumping waste, and bans on child labor, among many other criteria. Shoppers should be aware that as little as 30 percent of the beans in a bag have to be certified for the Rainforest Alliance label to be used. These certifications are expensive for farmers.

MICROLOT

A microlot is a batch of coffee processed at the same time and kept separate from other batches. For example, a farm may pick fifteen rounds of coffee during the harvest season; if all of the coffee harvested on a particular day is processed together in a batch and kept separate from coffee picked and processed on another day, this is one kind of microlot. The term can also be applied to coffees from different farms that are processed together at a central processing station on the same say.

When coffee estates grow multiple coffee varietals, they sometimes harvest and process the varietals separately, creating a varietal-specific microlot. Some estates also occasionally harvest coffees from particular areas of their farms with unique microclimates and process the cherries separately to create micro-microlots.

PROCESSING

Processing is often the most important factor in the flavor of coffee. At its simplest, the term refers to the removal of the pulp of the coffee cherry from the seeds we know as coffee beans. It used to be that most coffee, even the best stuff, was mixed together at central processing stations. By the 1990s many importers and other coffee buyers were asking for the highest-quality coffees to be processed separately. This led to an overall increase in the quality and accessibility of top-end specialty coffees. Conversely, some midlevel specialty coffees, now absent the highest-quality beans, declined in quality.

Natural

Natural (or dry) processing is the simplest, least expensive method. The coffee fruit is laid out on sunny patios or raised netted beds and allowed to dry. Because the fruit stays on the bean for a long time, naturally processed coffee often tastes intensely sweet, wild, and fruity (often blueberry- or strawberry-like). After shriveling and drying for two to four weeks, the coffee is sent off to mills where the dried fruit is removed from the beans. Although natural processing is traditional in dry countries like Ethiopia and Brazil, humid countries such as Costa Rica and Guatemala have been experimenting with it, with interesting results. Since naturally processed coffees are more prone to problems like overfermentation, coffee buyers sometimes consider them a riskier investment than washed or pulped natural coffees.

Washed

Washed (or wet) processing imparts consistently clear, clean flavors and good acidity that many roasters prefer. The fruit around the bean is stripped off soon after harvest using water or machines. The sticky pulp that remains, called mucilage, is removed either through fermentation or mechanically, and is washed off in channels of clean water. Once the beans are clean, they dry on sunny patios for a few days and then usually go into mechanical driers. Once dry, they rest for a couple of weeks before being sent to the dry mill to be bagged and exported. Thanks to water-saving technologies, washed coffees are beginning to appear in dry parts of the world.

Pulped natural

Pulped natural (also known as seminatural or honey) processing splits the difference between natural and washed processing. The fruity pulp is removed from the bean, but the mucilage is left on to dry in the air and sun. Coffee processed this way tastes clean but also has some of the sweetness or fruitiness of naturally processed coffee.

SEASONAL

In the most basic sense, coffee is seasonal because it only grows during defined seasons, which are different depending where you are in the world (for example, in Guatemala the harvest season is roughly December through March). But the word *seasonal* is often used to refer to the freshness of a coffee after processing. From the moment of harvest, the clock begins ticking on the shelf life of green, unroasted coffee. Many roasters adjust their menu according to the harvest seasons and try to only present coffees at their peak.

Seasonality is one reason you may not be able to find your favorite beans during certain months. Or why the flavor of your favorite blend suddenly changes—some of the coffee in it may go out of season and need to be replaced with a different coffee. Used in the sense of freshness, *seasonal* usually refers to coffee that has been roasted within six months of harvest. For peak taste, freshness does matter. Past-crop coffees often taste more woody, the flavor dulled.

SINGLE ORIGIN

Unlike a blend, which may contain coffees from all parts of the world, a single origin comes from one country and might be labeled, for example, "Guatemala." Though the concept of single-origin coffee is an old one, the term didn't come into widespread use until around the turn of the twenty-first century. Prior to that time, most coffee sold in stores was either unspecified and blended (remember breakfast blends?) or identified by country, port, or large geographic region. Contemporary roasters are more interested in the unique qualities of different coffees and identify them to the most precise unit possible, frequently to a single farm or co-op.

VARIETAL

Although older coffee companies may discuss varietals interchangeably with single origins (as in "Varietal: Guatemala"), the term has a more specific, useful meaning. Also called cultivars or varieties, varietals are the biological variations of different coffee species. Yellow Bourbon, Caturra, and Pacamara are all varietals of *Coffea arabica*, or arabica coffee. The varietal can have a profound impact on flavor, but not all coffees are identified or separated by varietal (some farms grow only one varietal of coffee, while others grow hundreds all mixed together). Arabica coffee is widely considered to be higher quality than robusta coffee (*Coffea canephora*), the other main species of the coffee trade. All of the roasters profiled here focus primarily on arabica coffees.

Coffea arabica includes hundreds of varietals, each with unique attributes that influence flavor, complexity, and yield.

A MATTER

OF

Taste

COFFEES are less generic and more unique than ever, a fact that roasters and cafés are keen to highlight. An easy way to start understanding variations in taste is to sip coffees side by side, the way you might with wine. But how are they different to begin with? If you've ever heard a coffee lover wax poetic about a "classic Guat," you've had a (mildly annoying) introduction to the idea of origin flavor. The best example of origin flavor may be coffee from the Harrar region of Ethiopia—even people who swear they can't detect any differences among coffees can pick up the intense blueberry taste.

Blueberries may be well and good, but what about "rose marmalade," "toasted Rolos," or, my personal favorite overwrought flavor description, "vintage '96 Cristal champagne"? Does coffee ever actually taste like these things? Roasters do take a bit of poetic license when describing their coffees. But I have certainly sipped coffee that tasted like a combination of sweet milk chocolate and slightly smoky caramel—something close to "toasted Rolos."

The word *taste* is somewhat misleading. A big part of tasting coffee is feeling it—the heaviness of it (body), the texture (mouthfeel), the way it lingers in your mouth after you've swallowed (finish). Much of the taste also comes from aroma—around a thousand volatile aromatics contribute to the complex flavors of coffee.

The more coffee you drink—and more importantly, the more you think about what you're drinking—the more conscious you become of differences in taste. Resist judging yourself pretentious and close your eyes when taking a sip. It will help keep the focus on what's going on in your mouth.

So what makes Ethiopian Harrar taste like blueberries? A few main factors collectively make up the origin character of a coffee: *terroir*, varietal, ripeness, and above all, processing methods. There are, of course, other critical aspects to the flavor of coffee, but origin character is immensely satisfying to explore. If you know a little about where coffee comes from, you can have a lot more fun drinking it and hone in on flavors and regions you prefer. A Guatemalan coffee is usually much more like another Central American coffee than an African or Indonesian one. If you know you like Guatemalan coffee but there isn't one on the menu, try something from Costa Rica. It will be different but in the same league. Coffee flavor is also affected by how ripe the coffee cherry was when it was picked (the riper the cherry, the sweeter the coffee) and how the coffee was roasted (see "Roast Craft" for more on this).

This chapter focuses on the flavor profiles of major origins, but it is worth noting that coffee enthusiasts are also increasingly interested in mapping microregions and studying how they affect flavor (much like the appellation system in wine). As many countries produce increasing amounts of unique, high-grown, farm-specific coffees—and as growers and roasters collaborate to experiment with traditional practices—it becomes more challenging and interesting to describe a type for any country.

TERROIR
elevation 1200-2500m
Hot
humidity
shade
defined rainy season
soil

RIPENESS
ripe—sweet, complex

PROCESSING
wet—clean, floral, bright
dry—fruity, sweet

SOUTH AMERICA

BRAZIL. About 25 percent of the world's total production of coffee is grown in Brazil (much of it robusta coffee, *Coffea canephora*). Brazilian coffee has a reputation for poor quality. Nevertheless, some treasures can be had from smaller farms that take care with their harvesting and processing. A classic Brazil is sweet and mild with a resonant chocolaty or nutty flavor (like a coffee peanut butter cup). These coffees are the traditional base for espresso blends, creating a platform from which more charismatic coffees can launch. Brazils are generally lower-grown, often in full sun, and are usually naturally processed (but also undergo pulped natural processing).

COLOMBIA. Americans associate coffee with Colombia more than any other place, largely due to a marketing coup on the part of the Colombian coffee board (with help from a certain mule). Many of the most exciting high-altitude coffees are Caturra (good acidity with medium body) and Typica (sweet and clean), with flavors ranging from mild earthen nuttiness to vivid cranberry tang.

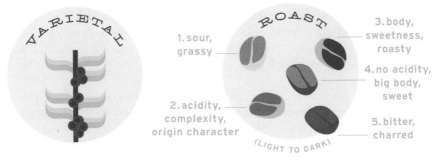

The flavor in a cup of coffee is influenced by five main factors, with processing method the single biggest determinant.

Caturra—bright, low body
Bourbon—sweet, balanced
Typica—clean, sweet
Geisha—complex, sparkling

VARIETAL

ROAST

1. sour, grassy
2. acidity, complexity, origin character
3. body, sweetness, roasty
4. no acidity, big body, sweet
5. bitter, charred

(LIGHT TO DARK)

CENTRAL AMERICA

COSTA RICA. These coffees are grown on high hillsides in humid climates and are notable for their clarity and balanced fruity acidity (despite the stereotype that Costa Rican coffee is boring or too mild). Most are wet-processed. An increasing amount of Costa Rican coffee is now milled on the farm where it was grown, meaning farmers have control over more of the process. This allows for some experimentation (as with forays into dry processing, which have had fascinating, fruity results).

EL SALVADOR. These coffees have come into their own. With two main varietals, Bourbon (classic, chocolaty) and Pacamara (bright, floral, creamy, unique), most great El Salvadors share the clarity of flavor that comes with wet processing.

GUATEMALA. Huehuetenango and Antigua are among the most popular coffee-growing regions in Guatemala, both at high elevations with cool weather and steady humidity. Guatemalan coffee, like any coffee from Central America, is generally washed because of the humidity, leading to good acidity and clear flavors. Guatemala is dominated by Bourbon, Caturra, and Typica varietals and is known for chocolate and fruit flavors and creamy texture.

AFRICA

BURUNDI. Coffee from Burundi is on the rise now that the higher-quality stuff can be separated out by regional washing stations. Primarily of the Bourbon varietal, Burundian coffee typically grows on small farms in the rich, volcanic soil of the country's many hills and mountainsides. More subtle than Kenyan coffee, but still with noticeable acidity.

ETHIOPIA. The birthplace of coffee and still home to some of the most interesting and alluring. Up to a thousand wild varietals grow in Ethiopia. Coffee from the Harrar region is dry-processed and boasts distinctive wild-fruit flavors (this is the "exploding blueberry" coffee) but can also have funky off-flavors. Coffee from regions like Sidama and Yirgacheffe is more often washed and is lighter in body with crisp acidity and floral notes—almost like tea.

KENYA. Thanks to an exceptional infrastructure for coffee, Kenya boasts overall good farming practices and superb coffee. Kenyans are distinctive for their complexity, acidity (lots of it), and berry-like juicy quality. This is the coffee most often compared to wine. Kenya's alphabet soup of main varietals—especially SL28 and SL34—were created in research and development labs for complexity, brightness, and balance, giving them their telltale flavor. Almost no Kenyan coffee is certified organic.

INDONESIA AND ASIA

PAPUA NEW GUINEA. Grown by smallholders in the highlands that form the backbone of the island, the best Papua New Guineas have delicate floral and citrus notes. These coffees are infinitely more refined than the throaty, musty-flavored Sumatrans and are often compared to Central American coffees.

SUMATRA. These profoundly distinctive coffees illustrate how processing methods affect flavor. In Sumatra, farmers use wet hulling, a unique, traditional method. Wet hulling gives a heavy body, very low acidity, and quirky flavors best described as earthy, mushroomy, winey, leathery, pipe-tobacco–like, or marijuana-like. Many people erroneously attribute the flavor to dark roasting.

Seed

TO CUP

THOUGH a good cup of coffee is one of life's simple pleasures, it contains a complex history. Coffee grows in the equatorial belt. It takes a coffee tree three to five years to produce coffee cherries. Once the coffee has been harvested, at least a month (sometimes many months) passes before it arrives in the United States. It's a minor miracle that we have the amazing coffee we do, given the journey it must take and all the things that could go wrong along the way.

This chapter provides a brief tour of that journey, beginning with a cup of coffee and working backward to show how it came to be and how long the process took.

RIGHT NOW: IN THE CUP

This is the part you already know. You're drinking a soul-warming cup of hot coffee. It has been brewed from ground, roasted coffee beans steeped in hot water. This cup of coffee took about four minutes to make, start to finish. It was made mere minutes ago.

What could go wrong: All manner of things. Preparing coffee isn't brain surgery, but it is famously easy to ruin even the best coffee through lack of attention, dirty equipment, or poor technique. Worst of all, you could simply forget to enjoy the little marvel in your cup.

HARVEST

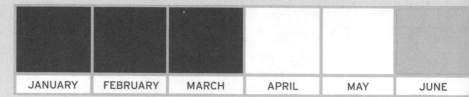

JANUARY	FEBRUARY	MARCH	APRIL	MAY	JUNE

JANUARY	FEBRUARY	MARCH	APRIL	MAY	JUNE

JULY	AUGUST	SEPTEMBER	OCTOBER	NOVEMBER	DECEMBER

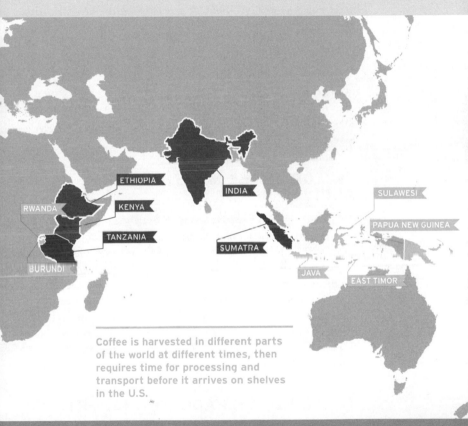

ETHIOPIA

RWANDA

KENYA

TANZANIA

BURUNDI

INDIA

SUMATRA

SULAWESI

PAPUA NEW GUINEA

JAVA

EAST TIMOR

Coffee is harvested in different parts of the world at different times, then requires time for processing and transport before it arrives on shelves in the U.S.

JULY	AUGUST	SEPTEMBER	OCTOBER	NOVEMBER	DECEMBER

AT MARKET

A FEW DAYS AGO: ROASTED

Let's say you're drinking this particular cup of coffee at a café run by an independent local roaster who is obsessed with freshness. The coffee you're drinking was roasted less than a week ago and stored in a dark, cool place.

What could go wrong: The roaster could ruin the beans by roasting them too light or too dark (or even set them on fire, though that rarely happens), or could blend coffees that don't complement each other. But to some degree these things are a matter of taste. What's not arguable is that roasted coffee should be used as soon as possible. Coffee tastes noticeably different ten days after roasting than it does three days after, due to gasses that continue to leave the roasted beans over time. After three weeks or so, coffee begins a long, slow descent toward the flavor of cardboard.

TWO OR THREE MONTHS AGO: ARRIVED IN THE U.S.

After their shipments arrive, roasters store green coffee and roast it as needed until it's gone. Some roasters buy enough to last an entire year so that they don't run out of a particular coffee, but that is becoming less common as roasters focus more on freshness and seasonality.

What could go wrong: There's no rule for how long green coffee remains fresh, but after perhaps a few months it will begin to taste a little like a paper bag or burlap—less sweet, more hollow, like the flavor is there but missing something. If it's stored properly, green coffee is generally okay for about eight months.

THREE MONTHS AGO: TRANSPORT

Green coffee can sit at a port in the exporting country for up to a month while customs paperwork and other details are worked out. It eventually comes to the U.S. via ship, which usually takes two to six weeks (or up to two to three months from Africa). After arriving at one of a handful of large ports, like Oakland or New York, the coffee travels to its final destination by train or truck.

JOURNEY OF THE BEAN

Coffee gets picked, crushed, dried, lifted, hoisted, roasted, and ground. Every step along the way can affect its flavor.

3 YEARS AGO

PLANTING

5 MONTHS AGO

HARVESTING

PROCESSING

DRYING

MILLING

RESTING

EXPORTING

SHIPPING

ARRIVAL

A FEW DAYS AGO

ROASTING

RIGHT NOW

BREWING

What could go wrong: Almost anything, which is what makes this the scariest part of the journey. The coffee could sit on a 120° tarmac, slowly cooking while it waits to be shipped. It could be placed in the wrong spot on a ship and sit in front of a diesel exhaust pipe for three weeks (nothing like the aroma of diesel in your morning cup). Experienced importers and exporters are critical at this stage, fixing problems as they come up and keeping everything moving.

FOUR MONTHS AGO: MILLING

Milling is the last step of grinding the final layer (parchment) of dried coffee fruit off the bean. It usually happens at large, central locations operated by exporting companies, near where the coffee will be bagged and shipped.

FOUR MONTHS AGO: RESTING

Ideally coffee is rested before it is milled, to help extend shelf life (without resting, beans go stale faster). During this intentional waiting period, the beans mellow and settle in huge mounds within protected warehouses. Resting generally takes two to four weeks, sometimes up to two to three months.

What could go wrong: If humidity in the warehouse isn't controlled, beans will take on a fermented taste. (In India, some coffee is "monsooned"—intentionally exposed to humid monsoon winds—to give it a mellow but wet-wool–like flavor, which would be considered a defect in other beans.)

FIVE MONTHS AGO: PROCESSING

Processing usually begins within minutes or hours of when coffee is harvested, and may take four to six weeks to complete depending on the method (natural, washed, or pulped natural—see "The Lingo" for a full description of each). In some locations, processing takes place right on the farm and then coffee makes its way to the port; in others, it happens at central locations.

What could go wrong: The dozens of variations on each processing method come with their own dangers. Naturally processed coffees are easily ruined if unexpected rains blow in or if they are not carefully tended—the sugary fruit could attract mold, ferment, or even rot. Wet-processed coffee is easier to control but can be ruined if allowed to overferment. Coffees badly ruined during processing generally do not make it into your cup but are sold for low prices and diverted elsewhere. Mildly defective coffees often end up in blends, where the off-flavors are not as noticeable.

FIVE MONTHS AGO: HARVESTING

Like the vegetables in your garden, coffee doesn't ripen all at once, so it's ideally picked multiple times each season. Since a lot of coffee is grown on steep mountainsides, often on small farms, it is usually picked by hand.

What could go wrong: Most farms can't afford the most ideal harvesting practices, which are labor intensive, so the majority of coffee is picked while not at absolute peak ripeness, leading to less natural sweetness and complexity in the cup.

THREE OR MORE YEARS AGO: PLANTING

Coffee plants reach maturity and bear fruit after about three to five years. Many of the biggest factors affecting a coffee's flavor have to do with the sapling the farmer planted in the ground. What varietal was it? In what quality soil? On what side of a mountain slope? Was it planted in the shade of a mango tree or in full sun?

What could go wrong: Poor irrigation, inadequate soil nutrients, and weather that is too hot, cold, rainy, or dry can all lead to sick trees. One result may be inferior quality, but compromised yields are even more damaging for the farmer, who is paid by the pound.

ROAST

Craft

THE COFFEE roaster is
the closest most of us will ever get to where
our coffee comes from. Contemporary
roasters take the role very seriously—
tinkering, playing, and experimenting in
the name of pushing at the boundaries of
what's possible. The caffeine addicts
profiled in this book—and coffee people
everywhere—are as hooked on the elegant intricacies of roasting as
they are on coffee's stimulating effects.

What are the essentials of roasting? It's pretty simple stuff: time, heat, movement, and of course coffee. Roasting is just a fancy word for cooking over fire. One kind of coffee roaster—the machine that cooks coffee—is a technology. The other roaster—the person in charge of the machine—is a manual tradesperson and professional taster. The sensory experience of creating roasted coffee, using sight, smell, and sound, is what occasionally elevates this craft to an art form, and what draws coffee roasters back to the physically demanding work every day.

SNAP, CRACKLE, CRACK

There is first of all sound: a cracking noise made when internal heat causes the moisture in a coffee bean to expand until it pops. Cracking happens in two stages: first crack and second crack. Coffee is done sometime around second crack, depending on the degree of darkness for the beans (well before second crack is generally considered a light roast, just before second crack is medium, and during or after second crack is dark). Sight and smell are intertwined as the roaster constantly checks the progressing roast to view its color and aroma. Over the course of eight to twenty minutes, the green bean is transformed from an agricultural product, smelling of hay and grass, to a cultural one: roasted coffee, ready for our daily rituals.

LIGHT VERSUS DARK

Coffee, like many things, is vulnerable to trends. Dark-roasted coffee has long been called strong, evoking an eternal American virtue. But dark roasting has also come under fire, some calling it a ploy to hide the flavor of cheap, low-quality beans. A counter-trend, toward extremely light roasting, has prevailed among some roasters.

Coffee can be roasted so lightly that it tastes like hay or grass, and can be roasted so darkly that it tastes burnt. Between the two extremes lies endless variety. Lighter roasting brings out more acidic (think fruity) flavors and some of the natural sugars in the coffee bean. Roast a little darker, and the flavors of the roast itself—namely caramelizing sugars—begin to dominate. All roasters try to dial in the roast to bring out the best expression of each coffee's unique characteristics, including the varietal, processing method, and region or elevation where it's grown.

LIGHT. Common names for light roasts include light cinnamon, cinnamon, New England, and light city. The origin character comes through, with bright acidity; natural sugars are evident, and the coffee often has a fruity or floral taste. Light roasts have low body. The beans are the color of milk chocolate, their surfaces free of oil. This is generally an undesirable roast for espresso, which needs strong body and more sugars to balance the natural acids.

MEDIUM. Roasts in this category are called American, city, and full city. Spice and sweetness balance the natural acidity; the origin character comes through but with noticeable roasty flavors. Medium roasts have more body than light roasts. The beans are a semisweet-chocolate color, with a hint of oil on the surface.

DARK. These roasts have many names: continental, light French, southern Italian, Vienna, full French, northern Italian, Spanish. Dark-roasted coffee has lots of roasty flavor and little or no origin character. If the beans are roasted very dark, the flavor will be smoky or burnt. Dark roasts have heavy body, but extremely dark roasts have very little body because many of the coffee's oils and solids have burned up. The beans are dark-chocolate-colored or black, with oil on the surface.

INTO THE FIRE

Roasters, like chefs, are constrained by their ingredients and their tools. They approach different coffees differently, considering each coffee's varietal and origin, how it was harvested and processed, the size of the beans and their moisture content. A roaster's main tool is the roasting machine. This can be a drum roaster, which roasts beans in a metal drum spinning over a flame, or a fluid air bed roaster, which floats the coffee on a bed of hot air (think of a plug-in popcorn popper). Drum machines are vastly more common among smaller roasters (including most of the companies profiled in this book), perhaps in part because of their nostalgic aura; the basic technology for drum roasters has not changed in over two centuries and is tightly coupled with the idea of the roaster as an artisan. Drum roasters cook more slowly and give a rounded flavor, generally with less acidity. They are better at imparting the roasty flavors of caramelizing (and sometimes burning) sugar, but many small roasters regularly produce beautiful light- or medium-roasted beans on drum roasters. Fluid beds were introduced in the 1920s and are popular for producing brighter flavors.

BLENDS

Coffee roasters also mix coffees into blends, an extremely difficult art form. Blending is a way for roasters to create consistency (since

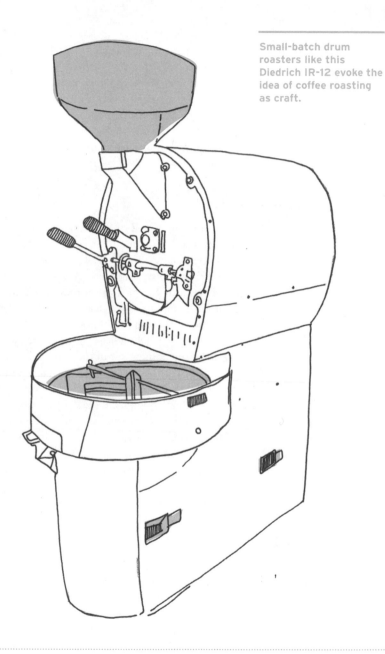

Small-batch drum roasters like this Diedrich IR-12 evoke the idea of coffee roasting as craft.

individual coffees are often unavailable year-round) and make a unique imprint. Some roasters are synonymous with their signature blends. Most great blends create a harmonious single impression despite having up to a dozen coffees in them (West Coast roasters usually use far fewer). Some blends contain as few as two coffees, the point being to help you tease out the unique flavor of each. For the balance they provide, blends are generally the first choice when making espresso. They usually consist of a base coffee that provides structure and mellow flavor, layered with more interesting coffees.

BEAN TOWNS

Seattle, a coffee city with deep history, likes its beans roasted darker, with a steadfast emphasis on espresso and blends. Portland and San Francisco have helped create a West Coast style, emphasizing single-origin coffees from small, traceable farms or mills, roasted lighter to bring out the unique flavors of where the coffee comes from. Anywhere that people drink coffee in the car (namely the suburbs), more darkly roasted coffees rule, geared to stand up to large quantities of milk. But exceptions are everywhere. The beauty of coffee today is that the choices are almost dizzying, from strong and bitter, to fruity and tealike, to chocolaty and nuanced.

Roast

YOUR OWN

COFFEE roasting is surprisingly easy, about as hard as popping popcorn or toasting nuts (and significantly easier than making cookies). The hard part is doing it really well. The roasters profiled in this book are dedicated craftspeople with a lot of experience and some special equipment. Roasting your own even once, just for fun, will deepen your appreciation for both coffee and the talented roasters who elevate the beverage to an art form. With that goal in mind, this chapter explores three ways to try roasting at home using simple, inexpensive equipment.

Another benefit of home roasting, if you really get into it, is financial. Depending on quality, green coffee beans may cost a third to half as much as what you'd pay at a shop counter. If you drink a half pound of coffee a week and normally spend $10 to $12 per pound, you could save $100 a year or more roasting your own. And since you probably won't roast more than you can drink in a week or so, you will always have fresh coffee.

Before you start experimenting, you'll need to know a bit about what to expect. First, to roast coffee you have to use very high temperatures, which means you're going to produce smoke—a lot of it. Set up your work area under an oven vent, near an open window with a fan, or best of all, outside. You'll need good-quality oven mitts or other protective gear to safely handle all hot surfaces. Naturally, since heat is involved, you'll also have to pay close attention to what you're doing—don't wander away while the coffee is roasting.

As coffee roasts, it expands. Chaff, a thin, papery inner skin of the bean, flakes off (think of the skin on a peanut). A batch of roasting coffee can produce a lot of chaff. It's fine if some of it stays stuck to the bean, but it can be messy.

Roasted coffee benefits from a short resting period before you drink it. After you've roasted and cooled the beans, put them in a container (a glass jar works great), but don't seal it until the next morning. This allows CO_2 created during roasting to dissipate.

ROASTING IN A STOVETOP POPCORN MAKER

STOVETOP POPCORN MAKER
½ POUND GREEN BEANS
KITCHEN THERMOMETER
STOPWATCH
METAL COLANDER

Roasting with a stovetop popcorn maker is the most hands-on method and creates a heavy-bodied roast.

Roasting with a Whirley Pop or other stovetop popcorn maker is a good approximation of how coffee would have been roasted on a homestead in the early nineteenth century. You can roast up to half a pound of coffee this way, and you'll get a full-bodied, medium-dark roast. This method produces a lot of smoke, so adequate ventilation is doubly important. It also requires constant attention (and churning) for about 15 minutes.

Let the coffee continue to rest one or two days before you drink it. Different coffees have different sweet spots, so you may decide you like one coffee best the day after it's roasted or on day five.

1. Set the empty popcorn maker over low-medium heat. Use a kitchen thermometer to monitor the temperature inside the popper. When it hits 400°F, reduce the heat to keep the temperature from rising too fast. The goal is to stabilize it at around 475°F.

2. Start the stopwatch. Pour the beans into the popper and begin cranking at a slow but steady pace. The temperature will drop when the cool beans are added and then begin to heat up again. Don't stop churning.

3. At 5 to 6 minutes you should hear a cracking noise like popcorn popping and begin to see smoke. This is first crack. (If you haven't heard it yet, the roast is too slow; plan to set your burner a little higher next time.) Wait about a minute, and reduce the heat to slow the roast.

4. At 10 to 12 minutes you'll hear a second, sharper set of cracks. Take the beans out now for a solid medium-dark roast. You can take them out earlier, at 8 or 9 minutes, for a lighter, brighter-flavored roast, or after second crack has ended for a pungent, roasty flavor.

5. Pour the extremely hot beans into the metal (not plastic!) colander when they are slightly lighter in color than desired (they will keep cooking until completely cool). Swirl them in the colander under a vent or in front of a window until they are warm to the touch. Chaff will fall off, so do this over a sink or bowl.

ROASTING IN AN ELECTRIC AIR POPCORN MAKER

**AIR POPPER
½ CUP GREEN BEANS
STOPWATCH
METAL COLANDER**

Air poppers roast the fastest and are good for lighter roasts.

Roasting coffee to a medium color in an air popper will give it a lovely, sweet, bright flavor. Use a popper that heats from vents on the side of the chamber, not the bottom (safe models include West Bend Poppery II, Kitchen Gourmet, Presto PopLite, and Nostalgia Brand). This recipe calls for ½ cup of green beans, but check the manufacturer's instructions for maximum amounts and adjust accordingly.

Though air poppers produce less smoke, you will still need to work near a window or vent. Note, too, that chaff will spurt out of the machine as the coffee roasts. To minimize the mess, roast outside.

1. Add the beans, and turn the machine on.

2. Start the stopwatch. After about 3 minutes you'll smell coffee smoke and hear the crackle of first crack. Check the color of the beans to see your progress.

3. For a lighter roast, take the beans out at 4 to 5 minutes. Remove them at 5 to 6 minutes for a medium roast, and 6 to 7 minutes for a medium-dark roast.

4. Turn the machine off, and pour the beans into the colander when they are slightly lighter than the color you want. Swirl them in the colander in a ventilated area until they are warm to the touch.

ROASTING IN AN OVEN

Oven roasting is tricky but fun—if you leave the oven light on, you can watch what's happening.

Think of oven roasting coffee as baking yourself breakfast. It's about as simple as making banana bread, and just as tasty, especially if you like your coffee roasted a little on the dark side. You'll want to use a gas oven, preferably convection (sorry, electric oven owners!). The recipe calls for 1 to 2 cups of beans, but the idea is to use enough for a single layer to cover the perforated part of whatever pan you use. A pan meant for crisping breads or pizzas should do nicely, especially one with raised sides, which will help keep the coffee from falling off.

Ovens roast coffee unevenly (because the beans are not in motion), which makes it hard to tell when you should call it done. The beans around the outer edges of the pan roast first, while those in the middle remain light. Make sure you can vent the smoke from your oven effectively. No two ovens cook alike, so use the temperatures here as a guideline and adjust accordingly. If your coffee is smoking heavily at 8 minutes, try a lower temperature. A finished roast should take 10 to 15 minutes, making oven roasting the slowest method.

GAS (PREFERABLY CONVECTION) OVEN
1 TO 2 CUPS GREEN BEANS
PERFORATED BAKING PAN
STOPWATCH
METAL COLANDER

1. Set a rack on the middle shelf of the oven, and preheat to 475°F convection / 500°F conventional.

2. Spread the beans evenly in the pan to form one layer, and place the pan in the oven.

3. Start the stopwatch. You should hear first crack at 5 to 7 minutes, as the coffee starts turning brown. Use the oven light (or a flashlight) to check the color of the roast.

4. If you prefer a brighter coffee, remove the pan at 8 minutes; for a medium-dark roast, take the beans out at the beginning of second crack, 9 to 11 minutes; for a darker, roastier flavor, remove it when second crack is well underway, at 12 or 13 minutes. This can be tricky because some of the beans in the center may still be in first crack when those at the outer edges are beginning second crack. Uneven roasts are perfectly fine and can add to the complexity of flavor. I prefer to take my coffee out just as second crack is beginning for the outer beans on the pan.

5. Pour the beans into the colander when they are slightly lighter in color than desired (you might want to use a metal funnel to help with this), and swirl them under a vent or in front of a window until they are warm to the touch. Be sure to have something on hand to catch the chaff that will fall as you do this.

COFFEE

AT

Home

IT'S PRETTY easy to destroy a great coffee at home, but perhaps a bit harder than the League of Connoisseurs would have you believe. You can do a number of small things to make yourself the tastiest possible cup of coffee, easily as good as anything from a topnotch café. Every step described in this chapter leads incrementally toward greater nuance and complexity of flavor. You don't have to jump in all at once and invest in expensive equipment—just take one step at a time and have fun.

Buy the best coffee

Make sure your coffee has been carefully sourced, thoughtfully roasted, and packaged for freshness. Look for a roast date on the bag. If the coffee is more than a couple of weeks old, the flavor will be weaker. Buy less coffee (a pound or less) more often to keep it from going stale in your cupboard. Blends tend to be cheaper, but that doesn't mean they can't be fantastic. With coffee, you tend to get what you pay for, though there is a curve of diminishing returns when you get into very expensive coffees. I generally buy from local roasters and expect to pay $5 per pound over the generic grocery brands for very good, fresh beans to make at home (and more for special coffees). If you don't know what you like, ask a barista to recommend something.

Grind it fresh

Grind coffee right before you drink it. Using a blade grinder is fine, but you will notice substantial improvements with a burr grinder, which crushes beans into uniformly sized pieces. (Blade grinders slice the beans, so some particles are tiny while others are huge, meaning that some of the coffee overextracts and some underextracts, giving you a bitter cup.) Cheap (around $30) hand-crank burr grinders are great if you don't mind a little morning workout. Baratza makes a well-regarded, midpriced (from $100) automatic grinder.

Store it properly

Store coffee out of sunlight in a cool, dry place. Don't put it in the freezer unless it's for long-term, one-time storage. Coffee beans break down in the face of constantly fluctuating temperatures, resulting in subpar, flat flavor. (You wouldn't repeatedly defrost and refreeze meat, would you?)

Use clean equipment

The oils in coffee go rancid over time. If you don't clean your equipment, those oils will come back to haunt you. Cleanliness is one reason some people prefer pour-over methods over French presses, which create a mess that is tantalizingly easy to leave until the next morning. French press is great; leaving cleanup for the next morning is grody.

Brew at the right temperature

Many of the beneficial acids in coffee (those that give great beans their zingwow factor) only come out of hiding at high temperatures, about 195°F–205°F. If you brew with cooler water, you'll sacrifice complexity. If you use water that is boiling hot, you'll burn the coffee, making it bitter and lackluster. Boiling water, counting to forty, and then pouring will get you roughly the right temperature. Most auto-drip coffee makers only heat to about 180°F, though some have temperature controls, like the Technivorm. Some electric kettles come preprogrammed with the right temperatures for coffee.

Don't buy pods

Yes, single-serving coffee pods are convenient, but they are tremendously wasteful, generally contain low-quality coffee, and are only produced and distributed by huge companies that charge unbelievable markups for the convenience. Cultivate your love of coffee by trying several small, local roasters instead. Go to a café and try something you've never had before. Or try one of the methods described in this chapter to make yourself a great cup of coffee by hand. It only takes a few minutes for a rewarding cup.

How much does it cost?

Honestly, you could make decent coffee with an old T-shirt and hot water. But you'll probably want to invest in some basic equipment, like a grinder ($30 to $200) and a French press ($20 to $80) or one-cup-at-a-time brewer that sits on top of a mug ($5 to $50). Beyond that the only cost is the coffee itself. A pound of coffee will make about twenty to thirty cups, so even an expensive bag of beans will average out to less than a dollar a cup—less than what you'd pay at a gas station and infinitely better.

MAKE IT

There are many great, inexpensive ways to make coffee at home, ranging from fully automatic to all-hands-on-deck, with each method affecting the ultimate flavor and body. If you're making a single mug (my favorite mug holds about 10 ounces), use 16 to 18 grams of coffee (2 to 3 tablespoons, or one standard coffee scoop). For a larger pot, use 55 to 60 grams of coffee to a liter of water (about 34 ounces). Let your taste buds be your guide: if you like coffee stronger, add more; if you like it weaker, use less.

auto-drip

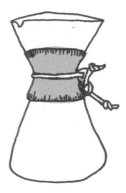

Chemex

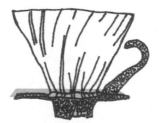

Hario V-60

Melitta

Kyoto-style cold
coffee dripper

Pour-over brewers

Many brewing methods are variations on pour-over, a timeless, versatile, easy-as-pie approach that is experiencing a renaissance. This method is as simple as it sounds: pour water over coffee in a filter, and it drips into a cup below. (The auto-drip is basically an automated pour-over.) Many cafés now feature pour-over bars where cups of coffee can be made by hand. Different brands of paper or metal filters catch oils a little differently, though most are roughly the same.

The trick to getting a great cup from pour-over is having the right amount of ground coffee at the right thickness, and pouring slowly—it should take about two to three minutes for the water to drip all the way through. If you are making a single cup of coffee, choose from the many variations on single-cup brewers, made from plastic, ceramic (my preference), and glass. To make a larger amount, try the Chemex, an elegant glass brewer that has endured since the 1940s.

Perhaps the most beautiful machine for making pour-over coffee is also the most unusual—a Japanese invention for preparing iced coffee, the Kyoto-style cold coffee dripper. Single drops of room-temperature water are released through a maze of glass tubes onto waiting coffee grounds. The process takes fourteen hours, and the resulting delicate brew is served over ice. The brewers aren't generally used at home but instead can be found at a handful of top cafés.

In preparing your own pour-over coffee, you generally want a medium grind. If the water passes through very quickly and the coffee tastes weak, use a finer grind. If the water is unable to pass through, use a coarser grind.

French press

French press

Clever Coffee Dripper

Eva Solo

siphon brewer

Immersion brewers

French press is the most common type of immersion brewer and is great for brunches, dinner parties, or any event where you need more than one cup. The main difference between it and any kind of pour-over is that with a French press the coffee grounds sit immersed in water for a relatively long period of time, generally leading to more body. Because the mesh filters in French presses have relatively large holes compared with a paper filter, more grit comes through (this is also partly why these brewers require a coarser grind). Many people love the chewiness a coffee gets when made in a French press. The Eva Solo immersion brewer is a prettied-up version of the same principle. The Clever Coffee Dripper looks like a pour-over brewer but actually works by immersion. Coffee sits in the brewer for four minutes, then you place it over a mug and a stopper is released, allowing the coffee to fall through a filter and into your cup. (The Clever is handy for making single cups using the immersion method, and because it uses a paper filter, it's easy to clean up.) Both the Eva Solo and the Clever produce a slightly cleaner-tasting cup than a French press.

Siphon brewers (also called vacuum pots) are close relatives of immersion brewers, but they produce an extremely clean cup of coffee. With their bulbous glass appearance and the fact that brewing occurs over either open flame or a futuristic halogen lamp, siphons appear to come straight out of a chemistry lab. Water is heated in a lower chamber, while ground coffee is added to the upper chamber. Some of the heated water turns to vapor, which expands and forces the remaining water to travel against gravity into the upper chamber. There, coffee steeps in the bubbling water. Heat is removed and the expanded hot air cools and contracts, allowing the brewed coffee to return to the lower chamber, passing through a filter on its way down. This is an enjoyable way to be served coffee in a restaurant, where tableside service allows dramatic brewing to play out in front of your eyes.

Plunge press

A relatively new type of brewer, the main plunge press on the market is the AeroPress, from the same inventor who created the Aerobie flying ring. This contraption gets points for being ugly while also making a fantastic cup of coffee. In an AeroPress, the coffee steeps in water and is then plunged through a filter that traps its oils. It makes a petite cup (about 6 ounces) and brews fast, in less than a minute. It's also an endlessly fun toy: add more or less coffee, try hotter or cooler water, try steeping for one minute or plunging right away, or flip it upside down and steep for four minutes before flipping it back and plunging. The brewed coffee grounds are easily popped out the end of the plunger for a low-hassle cleanup.

Aeropress

Moka pot

Many people think of coffee made with a moka pot as stovetop espresso because both methods produce strong, concentrated flavors and both rely on pressurized water for brewing. The steam pressure that occurs in a moka pot, however, is significantly less than what you find in a professional espresso machine, which means it doesn't produce anything quite like the flavors of real espresso. Traditional moka pot instructions emphasize using a fine, espressolike grind, but this generally makes a gnarly, bitter, overextracted coffee. Instead, use a medium-coarse grind, about the same as you'd use for drip coffee, and you'll be treated to a surprising, exciting cup.

Espresso makers

Making espresso at home can be extremely tasty and rewarding. You can make your own blends, try unique single origins, learn latte art. It can also be difficult and expensive. Espresso is an art built on a very specific technology—it doesn't scale down well,

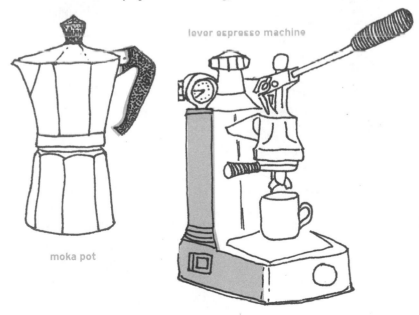

lever espresso machine

moka pot

and it takes a lot of practice. Cheap home espresso machines don't have enough oomph to make good foam for lattes and cappuccinos. Decent espresso machines can run into the many thousands of dollars, so you might have to drink ten shots a day for a couple of years to pay back the investment. A good-quality burr grinder is also essential and can cost up to a few hundred dollars. Dire warnings aside, making espresso at home is hella fun. A number of websites support home enthusiasts and supply home equipment for all levels of interest. And if you take espresso straight, consider getting an affordable, portable Mypressi Twist—it looks like an ice cream scoop on steroids, uses those cool nitrous oxide cartridges, and makes remarkably tasty shots. The lovely countertop Presso is another affordable, portable option requiring nothing more than access to boiling water.

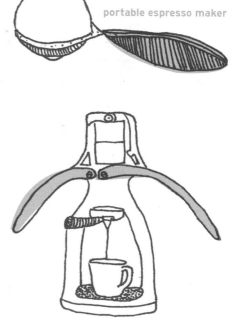

portable espresso maker

single-group espresso machine

manual espresso press

MAKING A STELLAR CUP AT HOME

*W*hen making coffee, some people prefer to measure by weight, others by volume. Measuring coffee by weight is more accurate, though measuring by volume (that is, by the spoonful) is more common. Professional baristas and serious enthusiasts often weigh the water for coffee instead of measuring it by volume, again for greater precision. For most people that's overkill, but for those interested in playing with the idea, I've included recommended water weight. Use a standard digital kitchen scale, and tare the weight of the cup or brewer before you begin. Note that 1 liquid ounce of cold water weighs 29.57 grams. ⟶

KEY

	GRIND:	
BREWER	fine	**NUMBER OF CUPS MADE**
RESULT	medium	**BREWING WATER**
COFFEE AMOUNT	coarse	**L** **BREW TIME**

POUR-OVER: MELITTA, HARIO, AND OTHERS

MAKES

1 mug, about 10 ounces

3 tablespoons or 18–20 grams

11 ounces or 325 grams

2½ minutes

Medium bodied, clean

SPECIAL STEPS

Rinse the paper filter if you are bothered by a papery taste. Soak the grounds with a little of the water, letting the coffee bloom for about 30 seconds, and then continue pouring slowly for 2 minutes.

POUR-OVER: CHEMEX

MAKES

3 mugs, about 32 ounces

8–9 tablespoons or 50–60 grams

34 ounces or 1000 grams

3½ minutes

Sometimes tea-like, very clean

SPECIAL STEPS

Pour the water in three parts. First, saturate the grounds to let the coffee bloom. Second, pour slowly, filling the filter to about ½ inch below the top. Third, after letting the water drain partway, slowly pour the rest of the water. If you are making a smaller pot of coffee, pour the water more slowly to give the grounds enough time to extract.

AUTO-DRIP

MAKES

4 mugs, about 40 ounces

 9-10 tablespoons or 68-75 grams

 42 ounces or 1240 grams

 4 minutes

Medium bodied, clean

SPECIAL STEPS

Brewed coffee left on a heated element will scorch and get bitter; pour it off into a thermos instead. Rinse your brewer thoroughly after every use.

IMMERSION: FRENCH PRESS

MAKES

3 mugs, about 32 ounces

 8-9 tablespoons or 50-60 grams

 34 ounces or 1000 grams

 4 minutes

Thick, full bodied, juicy, with chewy grit

SPECIAL STEPS

Pour half the water first, then stir the coffee and pour in the rest. Drink the coffee immediately, or pour it into a thermos (the grounds will continue extracting if you leave the water on them, making a bitter cup).

IMMERSION: EVA SOLO

MAKES

3 mugs, about 32 ounces

 tablespoons or 50–60 grams

 34 ounces or 1000 grams

 4 minutes

Full bodied, with less grit than a French press

SPECIAL STEPS

Put the ground coffee in the bottom of the carafe, and pour the water over it. Air pockets are easily trapped, so give the grounds a good stir. Zip up the thermal liner, and let the mixture steep. Make sure the mesh filter is in place before you pour. If you are making half a pot, halve the water and coffee amounts. (If the thermal sleeve is unzipped, pour the water until it reaches the top of the zipper; this is halfway full.)

IMMERSION: CLEVER COFFEE DRIPPER

MAKES

1 mug, about 10 ounces

 tablespoons or 18–20 grams

 11 ounces or 325 grams

 4 minutes

Full bodied without grit

SPECIAL STEPS

Rinse the paper filter if you are bothered by a papery taste. Keep the brewer on the counter while the coffee steeps. Stir the grounds about halfway through to ensure even extraction. When steeping is done, place the brewer on top of your mug; the drain valve will open automatically.

PLUNGE PRESS: AERO-PRESS

MAKES

1 short mug, about 6 ounces

2-3 tablespoons or 14–22 grams

Fill to the top of the chamber, 8 ounces or 235 grams

less than **1** minute

Full bodied, clean

SPECIAL STEPS

Assemble the two pieces of the plunger and insert the filter. Let the coffee steep in the water for 30 seconds to 1 minute, then plunge slowly. (Note that the manufacturer's unusual directions result in a less lively cup with little body. They call for brewing at double strength—using half the water—and then topping off your cup with hot water, as well as using water heated to 170°F.)

MOKA POT

MAKES

1 short mug, about 4 ounces

Fill to the top of the filter, about

10-11 grams

 6 ounces or 175 grams*

5 minutes

Full bodied, syrupy texture, very concentrated flavor

SPECIAL STEPS

Using a medium-coarse grind will produce a less bitter coffee than is traditional for this brewer. Pour the water into the bottom of the brewer, fill the basket with grounds, screw the pot together, and place it on high heat. Listen carefully to hear the coffee bubbling up. When the top chamber is half full, take the pot off the stove and let it finish filling. Serve right away.

*Do not exceed the safety line.

Northern California has been bona fide coffee territory for a long time. Oakland hosts one of the largest shipping ports in the country and is a primary gateway for coffee beans to enter the U.S. Add a thriving artisan food-and-drink scene, and you have a recipe for coffee nirvana.

San Francisco is supposedly the birthplace of the latte and is certainly the site of some of the first espresso bars in the U.S. In the twenty-first century, the roasting community has grown by leaps and bounds. With their emphasis on traceably sourced, more lightly roasted, single-origin coffees, San Francisco's newer roasters share tastes with Portland to the north. But the Bay Area is unique in boasting a number of almost theatrically large, natty roastery-cafés. Thanks to an emphasis on the leading edge, few of San Francisco's newer roasters are interested in traditional practices for blending coffees for espresso, a notable paucity in an otherwise wonderful coffee town.

Beyond the Bay Area, great coffee roasters are scattered around the northern half of the state, including some genuine innovators and leaders, especially in the wine regions and coastal areas. The dry interior valley has fewer options, though more than you might imagine. Great coffee has also started popping up in Southern California, especially Los Angeles, where coffee culture is going gangbusters.

BLUE BOTTLE COFFEE

MODERN COFFEE IN GORGEOUS OLD SPACES

Blue Bottle is a well-known and ubiquitous artisan roaster in San Francisco with a collection of alluring cafés in the Bay Area (and a roastery and more cafés in New York). Each café employs the fruitful troika of beautiful location, thoughtful preparation, and exquisite packaging. No two look alike, and each offers exclusive coffees created for the unique feel of the place. The thread holding these charmingly split personalities together is a modern coffee experience served up in a gorgeous old space. At Mint Plaza, soaring ceilings let in crashing light while baristas in crisp aprons preside over elegant, high-tech gear, like a much-ballyhooed Japanese siphon bar. The café's house espresso is aptly named 17 Ft. Ceiling. The rooftop café at the San Francisco Museum of Modern Art offers desserts honoring the artists featured in the galleries (the Mondrian cake is a work of art), an exclusive SFMOMA espresso blend, and custom-designed ceramic cups. Meanwhile an elegant

ROASTERY AND TASTING ROOM:
300 WEBSTER ST., OAKLAND

ROASTING SINCE '02

5000–20,000 lb./week

on 22-kilo, 75-kilo Probat roasters

FIND THE COFFEE AT BLUEBOTTLECOFFEE.COM / THEIR TASTING ROOM /THEIR SF AND NYC CAFÉS

BLUE BOTTLE SHOWCASES COFFEE WITH STYLE, SERVICE, AND A LITTLE BIT OF SASS.

stack of bricks in Oakland contains the company's roastery, pastry kitchen, and cupping lab—the whole catastrophe. Separated by a wall of glass is a café, where you can order from a deep menu of blends, single origins, and special reserve lots. Or stop by for one of a regular series of coffee tastings (check the website for schedules).

A TINY PUFF OF COFFEE-SCENTED AIR

Blue Bottle's beginnings were less than glamorous. The original roastery, which opened in 2002, operated out of a tiny, 186-square foot potter's shed in Berkeley. However humble, it was an important milestone in founder James Freeman's lifelong obsession with coffee. Beginning at age four, Freeman found himself transported whenever he was allowed to open his parents' canister of MJB, which emitted a tiny puff of coffee-scented air. The memory of that scent eventually led him to roast his own beans, initially on an oven tray. At the time, Freeman was a professional classical musician sensing his career beginning to stale. Within a few short years he opened Blue Bottle with the promise of freshness, vowing to "only sell coffee less than forty-eight hours out of the roaster."

LARGE MENU OF (MOSTLY) ORGANIC BLENDS

At Blue Bottle, every cup of coffee is made by hand (they've used pourover bars from the beginning), and most of their coffees (90 percent, according to Freeman) are certified organic. They craft and maintain a large menu of blends. Most are medium roasted, like the popular Bella Donovan, which Freeman calls the "wool sweater" of the blend lineup—"warm, comforting, familiar." He describes other coffees with equal cleverness. Case in point, the Three Africans blend: "Unlike some of our Ferry Plaza Farmers' Market specials, which tend to be nichey and polarizing, this blend has a very easy-to-like personality, good body, unthreatening complexity, and reasonably clean aftertaste." The website provides a charming illustrated guide to making coffee at home, and they sell an equally charming coffee coloring book.

CAFFE TRIESTE

COFFEE HISTORY AND BEAT CULTURE CONVERGE AT CAFFE TRIESTE.

LEGENDARY HANGOUT FOR ARTISTS

When you walk into the original Caffe Trieste in North Beach, try not to trip over any mousy young men clutching dog-eared copies of *Howl*. Located just a few blocks from City Lights Bookstore—ground zero for the West Coast's Beat culture—the Italian-themed Trieste was a central hangout for writers like Jack Kerouac, Allen Ginsberg, Richard Brautigan, and Lawrence Ferlinghetti. Francis Ford Coppola hammered out much of his *Godfather* script here. The café has been memorialized in poems, photographs of its famous patrons (many of which hang on the wall), and documentaries galore.

FIRST WEST COAST ESPRESSO BAR

After moving his family to America from Italy, Giovanni "Papa Gianni" Giotta became frustrated by how hard it was to find a demitasse of the beloved Italian national beverage: syrupy sweet espresso. He opened the Trieste in 1956 as a gathering place for the city's substantial Italian immigrant community. Little did he know that his café, where he served his own dark-roasted coffees, would change American culture forever. Trieste is known as the first dedicated espresso café on the West Coast and is credited with popularizing the cappuccino in the U.S. (1956 price: $0.30). Though Papa Gianni never became the professional opera singer of his dreams, his family has been singing bel cantos, show tunes, and country and western songs in weekly shows at the café since 1971.

ORIGINAL CAFÉ: 601 VALLEJO ST., SAN FRANCISCO

ROASTING SINCE

'56

"Millions of cups a year"

on a 600 lb. Jabez Burns roaster

FIND THE COFFEE AT CAFFETRIESTE.COM / THEIR CAFÉS

A LIVING PIECE OF AMERICAN HISTORY

American poet laureate Joseph Brodsky wrote, in "Caffe Trieste: San Francisco," "Nothing has changed here. Neither the furniture nor the weather." He could have added "nor the coffee." The espresso roast at Trieste follows a strict formula that Papa Gianni once described as "set in stone." In a town flooded with quality-obsessed roasters, Trieste's bitter coffee isn't the draw. Rather, the company is a living part of the history of American art and American coffee. (Perhaps fittingly, it also played a more vexing role in the history of gourmet coffee—the idea for the flavored latte is said to have been born at Trieste when a young entrepreneur got the idea to add Torani Italian soda syrups to coffee. Since the 1980s, sugary, flavored, hot-milk drinks have been the vanguard of gourmet coffee, much to the chagrin of coffee innamoratos.)

DE LA PAZ COFFEE ROASTERS

DE LA PAZ CONNECTS THE FARM TO THE CUP.

GETTING TO KNOW (AND WOO) FARMERS

De La Paz is among a growing number of roasters building relationships with small farms and arranging regular trips to check in with growers. As relative newcomers to this way of sourcing coffee, the company remains in the getting-to-know-you phase, relying on brokers to help them become acquainted with farms. When they find coffees they love, next comes the hard work of wooing: traveling to farms to meet growers, learning about the back end of the coffee trade, maintaining transparency and trust. As De La Paz gets more serious about direct trade, they have a small leg up: in school, owner Jason Benford studied agro-ecology with a focus on coffee farms. He also speaks fluent Spanish, and his wife, MariPaz (whom the company is named after), is a translator, which makes courting coffee farmers—at least those in Latin America—a bit easier on the nerves.

72 PERCENT BLOOD ORANGE, 28 PERCENT CHOCOLATE NUZZLE

De La Paz prints the exact ingredients of their blends right on the bag (for example, 72 percent Kenya from the Kasinga co-op, 28 percent Brazil from the Chapadao de Ferro farm). Because they generally focus on single-origin coffees, blends are two- or three-ingredient affairs and lightly roasted. If it sounds unnecessary to know whether your espresso is 28 percent of anything, you may be right. But the idea is that with only a small number of coffees and good information about the blend, coffee drinkers can begin to recognize the unique flavors of each component—the bite of blood orange from the Kasinga, the chocolate nuzzle from the Chapadao de Ferro.

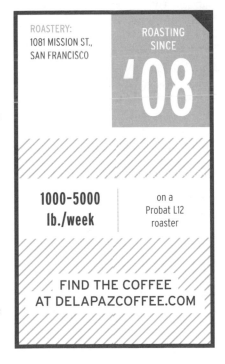

ROASTERY:
1081 MISSION ST.,
SAN FRANCISCO

ROASTING SINCE

'08

1000-5000
lb./week

on a
Probat L12
roaster

FIND THE COFFEE
AT DELAPAZCOFFEE.COM

ECCO ROASTING

CULINARY DELIGHTS OF COFFEE ROASTING

A gentle giant of the modern specialty-coffee world, founder Andrew Barnett's love of the beverage is straightforward. The company's original name says it all: Ecco ("here is") Caffe ("coffee"). Little tastes populate his day—an espresso here, a Brazilian single origin there. Barnett was a chef when he stumbled upon good coffee in the mid-1990s at Espresso Vivace in Seattle. Like the food he prepared, the coffee was fresh and obsessively crafted. Barnett began by shipping Vivace's coffee to his Sonoma café at the Western Hotel, but he soon became enraptured enough to start roasting his own, and eventually traded in his chef's knife for a full-time cupping spoon.

> LIKE A CALIFORNIA WILDFIRE, ECCO ROASTING CAME BLAZING FROM A QUIET CORNER TO BECOME A PREMIER AMERICAN ROASTERY.

STAND-OUT BRAZILIAN COFFEES

Ecco instinctively prioritizes taste over trends. Through Barnett, the company is credited with reintroducing boutique roasters to Brazilian coffees. Brazils have a reputation for being filler—unspectacular stuff best used as a cheap base for blends. In their least exalted state, Brazils can taste muddy, woody, and too mild, a result of being grown at low elevations on large tract

ROASTERY:
1125 MARIPOSA ST.,
SAN FRANCISCO

ROASTING
SINCE

'00

1000-5000
lb./week

on a
Probat UG22
roaster

FIND THE COFFEE
AT ECCOROASTING.COM
/ THEIR ROASTERY

TITAN-OWNED, WITH MORE CLOUT

In 2008 Ecco was bought by Chicago based Intelligentsia—or Intelli, in the parlance of the trade—which is frequently aligned with Stumptown and Counter Culture as one of the country's most influential boutique roasting companies. The deal gave Ecco the clout to buy high-quality coffees it was previously too small to access and gave Intelligentsia the ability to buy and feature small lots that would be too small for the larger brand. In general, the menus for the two brands are different, but occasionally some coffees show up on both (in the case of El Salvador Finca Matalapa, for example, each brand carried different lots from the same farm). Because Ecco and Intelligentsia use different roasters (the latter uses German Gothot machines) the same coffees may take on slightly different qualities.

farms without shade. In 2001 Barnett tasted a high-grown coffee from a farm called Vargem Grande. He was hooked. Fancy Brazils aren't the lurid, frilly coffees you might expect from the home of Carnival; they are clean and sweet, with balanced complexity, often with flavors of nuts, sweet fruit, and a hint of wood. Ecco continues to feature stand-out Brazilian coffees as single origins, now one among many roasteries to do so.

BAR CRAWL

*I*f you're in the mood for something special or just want to try something new, visit one of the growing number of coffee bars that feature beans from multiple roasting companies. Some focus on local roasters, while others highlight international boutiques. These cafés are run by coffee fanatics, with baristas who pay meticulous attention to detail. You are pretty much guaranteed a superior cup of joe.

CALIFORNIA

Ma'velous Coffee and Wine Bar,
1408 Market St., San Francisco, maveloussf.com
Drinking coffee at this high-gloss coffee and wine bar is an experience. Beans from local roaster Ecco Roasting are always on standby, as are those from Intelligentsia and Stumptown. Other roasters rotate through, including international superstars like Tim Wendelboe (Norway), Coffee Collective (Denmark), and 49th Parallel (Canada). Each coffee can be brewed in six different ways, using a one-of-a-kind espresso machine, manual brewers (Hario V60 drip, Chemex, or French press), a sophisticated Japanese siphon brewing machine, or the Kyoto-style slow-drip iced coffee maker.

CONTINUED >

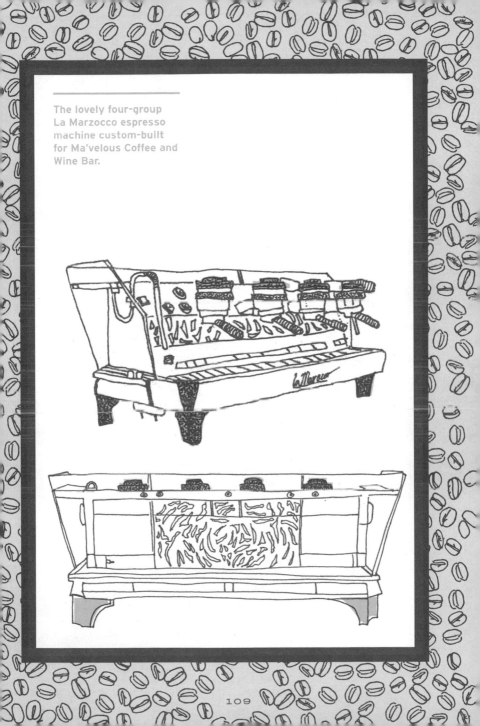

The lovely four-group
La Marzocco espresso
machine custom-built
for Ma'velous Coffee and
Wine Bar.

Modern Coffee
411 13th St., Oakland, moderncoffeeoakland.com
"Oakland's first coffee taproom" features Bay Area roasters
like Four Barrel, Sightglass, and Ecco.

Red Berry Coffee Bar
231 E Santa Clara St., San Jose, redberrycoffeebar.com
Smack in the middle of downtown San Jose (across from City
Hall), Red Berry serves coffee from Bay Area roasters like
Verve, De La Paz, and Temple.

OREGON

Barista
539 NW 13th Ave., Portland, 1725 NE Alberta St., Portland,
baristapdx.com
Owned by well-regarded West Coast coffee slinger Billy
Wilson, Barista was the first to operate on the multiroaster
model. Both locations, in the trendy Pearl and Alberta Arts
districts, are gorgeously appointed. Barista regularly
carries coffee from boutique roasters up and down the West
Coast and all across the country. It is often the only place in
Portland to try outstanding coffee from the East Coast, Deep
South, and Midwest.

WASHINGTON

Milstead and Co.
770 N 34th St., Seattle, milsteadandco.com
Barista Andrew Milstead opened Seattle's hottest mul-
tiple-roaster café in 2011 to much fanfare. The Fremont

neighborhood joint features coffee from Stumptown,
Intelligentsia, Coava, and the occasional Seattle roaster.

Onyx Coffee Bar
1015 Railroad Ave. #105, Bellingham, onyxcoffeebar.com
Onyx has a rotating selection of coffees on tap from up to a
dozen roasters from Los Angeles to Puget Sound, as well as
the occasional international roaster. Expect a coffee experience pared to its essentials: you'll find black coffee, prepared
as a pour-over (hot or iced) or as an espresso or Americano,
but no milk or sugar. Onyx is owned by Edwin Martinez, a
respected third-generation coffee grower who splits his time
between Bellingham and his family's farm in Guatemala,
Finca Vista Hermosa. His family's coffees are often available
at Onyx.

Tougo Coffee Co.
1410 18th Ave., Seattle, tougocoffee.com
A vibrant community café in Seattle's South Lake Union
neighborhood, Tougo offers coffees from Stumptown, Ritual,
and Velton's, among others. Featuring a deep menu of slow brew
methods like AeroPress, siphon, and V60.

FOUR BARREL COFFEE

HUGE CAFÉ WITH A MASCULINE VIBE

If Four Barrel added velvet ropes out front, its rustic-industrial gentlemen's club look would be complete. The manly, warehouse-sized café is made largely from reclaimed materials, including four stuffed boars' heads and tables consisting of 3-inch-thick slabs of wood bolted to the wall at right angles. Two separate bars add to the warehouse party aura. At the slow bar, order from a select list of single-origin coffees (espresso, Chemex, siphon, and so forth). For a regular cup of joe, or a latte, cappuccino, or any other drink made with house espresso, order at the main bar.

> FOUR BARREL IS THE PLAYBOY MANSION OF SINGLE-ORIGIN COFFEE.

SELECT SINGLE ORIGINS FROM THOUSANDS TASTED

Look past the bawdy show and you'll find one of the most serious coffee programs in the city. All three Four

Barrel coffee directors taste thousands of coffees a year (in Kenya, buyers taste up to 150 every day at a central auction lab), and all three have to agree about a coffee's Four Barrelness before purchasing it. In general they prefer washed beans grown at high elevations; these are clean, sweet, and balanced, with underlying complexity, letting *terroir* shine through. All Four Barrel coffees are bought to be showcased as single origins (even if some end up in the seasonally changing house blend), and most come from Latin America and Africa.

A UNIQUE ROAST FOR EVERY COFFEE

From a high counter at the back of the café, you can sip a single-origin cappuccino and watch the main show: men at work roasting coffee. Owner Jeremy Tooker believes the best roasting is done by calloused hands, not computers. The company's finely tuned, manually operated, vintage Probat is a source of immense

pride. On it, every coffee is roasted differently—no single play dominates the roasting playbook. Though Tooker resists terms like medium roast (too reductionist!), none of the coffees are roasted to second crack.

ROASTERY AND FLAGSHIP CAFÉ:
375 VALENCIA ST.,
SAN FRANCISCO

ROASTING SINCE
'08

5000-20,000 lb./week

on a Probat UG15 roaster

FIND THE COFFEE AT FOURBARRELCOFFEE.COM / THEIR CAFÉ

GRAFFEO COFFEE

COFFEE FOR THE ITALIAN COMMUNITY

Between World War I and World War II, sixty thousand boisterous Italian immigrants packed themselves into a few square blocks of San Francisco's North Beach neighborhood. They were masons, fishermen, scavengers, and produce mongers—and at least one coffee roaster. John Graffeo, originally from Sicily, sold fresh-roasted coffee to his motley neighbors from a little storefront on Columbus Avenue. The storefront is still there, and you can still walk in and buy a pound of the Graffeo blend. It's run now by Luciano Repetto, who has been roasting coffee in this exact spot since he was twelve years old, after his father bought the store in 1955.

ROASTING ON A BED OF HOT AIR

The Graffeo blend contains coffee from Colombia (for body), Costa Rica (for smoothness), and Papua New Guinea (for bite). The roasts are light and dark: the light is tangier, the dark smoother and a little sweeter. In early times, Graffeo used a traditional cast-iron drum to roast its small batches of coffee. But in the late 1970s, Repetto switched to fluid air bed roasting. The roasting machine is like a giant popcorn popper, holding coffee aloft on a bed of hot air. Coffee roasted on fluid air has more acidity and clarity of flavor, while drum roasters produce slightly more

> GRAFFEO KEEPS IT SIMPLE AND HONEST, WITH ONLY ONE BLEND ROASTED LIGHT AND DARK.

muddled, roasty flavors and more body. Fluid air bed machines lack the aura of craftsmanship of drum roasters, but that's just fine with Repetto, who believes coffee is more a technology than a mystery.

FROM SAN FRANCISCO TO SINGAPORE

Ironically, Graffeo is now easier to find in Asia than the U.S. The company licensed a separately run roasting facility in Singapore in 2003, which roasts coffee for luxury hotels across Asia. They feature the Graffeo blend as well as select lots of special single-origin coffees purchased at auction. In some ways that makes Graffeo Asia-Pacific more of a direct competitor with other Bay Area roasters than the U.S. Graffeo. But Repetto has no plans to change: many of his customers have been drinking "light" and "dark" for more than thirty years, all the evidence he needs that he's doing something right.

ORIGINAL ROASTERY AND STORE:
735 COLUMBUS AVE., SAN FRANCISCO

ROASTING SINCE '35

1000-5000 lb./week

on 50 lb., 175 lb. Sivetz fluid bed roasters

FIND THE COFFEE AT GRAFFEO.COM / THEIR ROASTERY-STORE / THEIR SAN RAFAEL STORE

RITUAL COFFEE ROASTERS

RITUAL OBSERVES THE RITES OF COFFEE WITHOUT BEING HEMMED IN BY TRADITION.

FLAGSHIP CAFÉ:
1026 VALENCIA ST.,
SAN FRANCISCO

ROASTING SINCE

'06

1000-5000 lb./week

on Probat L12, UG22 roasters

FIND THE COFFEE AT RITUALROASTERS.COM / THEIR BAY AREA CAFÉS

SIGNATURE SINGLE-ORIGIN ESPRESSO

Ritual's faux socialist logo (the bold red outline of a cup and a jaunty red star) hints at the company's idealism. It was among the first small roasteries in San Francisco to fully embrace the hyper-quality coffee movement, including its adoration of light-roasted single origins. The house espresso, Sweet Tooth, isn't a blend as you might expect, but a rotating single origin roasted just for preparation as espresso; it changes about once a month. It's just one example of owner Eileen Hassi's commitment to staying on the leading edge.

LONG-STANDING CONNECTIONS TO FARMERS

There's a heavy focus on so-called New World coffees, which tend to have the fruity flavors that Ritual's working-class heroes prefer. Coffees are roasted with a very light touch—some find them too bright or sour, while others love the glinting fruitiness. Ritual is all about agrarian ideals. The company sources nearly all of its coffee from farms it has built a direct relationship with (meaning buyers have either visited the farms and worked with the farmers or have worked with mill or co-op directors). In Costa Rica, for example, Ritual has worked closely with the Los Chacones farm, purchasing the entire harvest since 2008 and helping fund a long-term replanting project.

INNOVATIVE LOCATIONS FOR THE MASSES

The indie chain's newest café is a temporary pop-up shop built out of a shipping container, a form-meets-function embodiment of the farm-to-cup movement. (It's part of the Proxy Project, a galleria of foodie-in-a-box outlets in the Hayes Valley neighborhood.) Two permanent cafés, one in a floral shop and one in Napa's Oxbow Public Market, similarly play on the notion that coffee doesn't just materialize in your cup but comes out of the ground. The original Ritual café in the Mission District is the most traditional, the kind of place where you could sit and write a manifesto over an Americano. It opened in 2005, just as San Francisco was getting a taste for the young, brash, opinionated approach to coffee that Ritual serves up so adroitly.

SIGHTGLASS COFFEE ROASTERS

A WINDOW INTO COFFEE

In a 7000-square-foot former sign-manufacturing warehouse, brothers Jerad and Justin Morrison have created a café and roastery of ecclesiastical proportions. It took two years, a chunk of change, and dozens of dump trucks, but the monumental café in the SoMa district of San Francisco finally opened in summer 2011. A passion for transparency is evident throughout. The functional guts of the space are on display: an open roasting area, two bars (one an island, approachable from all sides), a floating mezzanine with seating and a cupping lab, lots of glass, and a bare-bones design approach. Even the company name is implicated, referring to the small window on a coffee roaster, the only part of the machine you can see through.

SIGHTGLASS IS FULLY INFUSED WITH MODERN IDEAS ABOUT COFFEE, NAMELY AN OBSESSION WITH TRANSPARENCY.

ROASTING TO REVEAL ORIGIN FLAVOR

"Light, bright, and exciting"—that's how the Morrisons describe their approach to coffee. The light roasting they embrace has swept through San Francisco like a brush fire. The brothers see it as an integral part of their commitment to transparency, roasting each coffee to bring out its origin characteristics (an awkward

ROASTERY AND
FLAGSHIP CAFÉ:
270 7TH ST.,
SAN FRANCISCO

ROASTING
SINCE

'10

1000-5000
lb./week

on a
Probat UG22
roaster

FIND THE COFFEE AT
SIGHTGLASSCOFFEE.COM
/ THEIR CAFÉ

tall order to expect the average coffee drinker to recognize, for example, a Sumatran coffee among four counterparts, but it's also a diverting way to test one's palate. At any rate it shakes up the well-worn idea that blends should create a harmonious single impression.

A COMPELLING BRAND

The Morrisons knew from the start they wanted to get people thinking about what makes coffee worshipworthy for them: fresh, single-origin beans that can be traced to small, quality-committed farms. Both have an intuitive sense about how to make people interested in, and covetous of, their wares. From the clean circular logo, to custom leather-and-denim barista aprons, to the industrial-warm aesthetic of the space itself, the style of Sightglass exerts a magnetic pull. You might not be able to pull your nose away from the glass.

metaphor for something you turn brown, but whatever). They like to purchase washed coffees with lots of citrus and fruit flavors, and feature them as single origins. But even the Owl's Howl seasonal espresso blend is part of the transparency conceit. The Morrisons want their customers to "see through" the blend to identify the flavor of each coffee in it. It's a

MR. ESPRESSO

FROM ELEVATORS TO ESPRESSO

Mr. Espresso is Carlo Di Ruocco, an elevator repairman who came to the U.S. from Salerno, Italy, in the 1970s. As Italian culture penetrated the Bay Area, Di Ruocco began to import and repair espresso machines for the Italian restaurants and cafés doing so well in the region. He soon became fed up with the severe, dark-roasted beans of the day, sharply unlike the sweet, mellow coffee of his home country. Drawing on the know-how he had acquired as a boy while working for a roaster in Italy, he bought himself an old-school, wood-fired coffee roaster and got to work.

OAK-ROASTED, SWEET, AND MILD

Wood-roasted coffee is both primal and romantic. At Mr. Espresso's Oakland roastery, flames lick at the bottom of a large cast-iron drum in which the coffee spins and cooks (neither fire nor smoke touches the beans). A wood-fired roaster is more like a cruise ship than a sailboat—it's hard to "turn" the roast (bringing the temperature up or down to fine-tune the flavor profile). The heat is controlled by the type and amount of wood used. It takes seven to eight pieces of hot, even-burning white oak to roast 500 pounds of coffee. According to head roaster John Di Ruocco, the relatively moist heat from wood (compared with gas) allows the coffee to be roasted more slowly. At Mr. Espresso, coffee des-

WITH WOOD AND FIRE, MR. ESPRESSO CHARTS A COURSE BETWEEN OLD WORLD AND NEW.

tined for espresso blends is roasted for twenty-two to twenty-four minutes. Despite the long roasting time, the Neapolitan blend has the appearance of a medium-roasted coffee, with a mild, pleasant flavor of caramelized sugars: sweet comfort in a cup. (When it was introduced in the early 1980s, the blend was significantly lighter than other coffees available in the Bay Area.) Single origins are roasted faster, about eighteen to twenty minutes, to preserve crisper acidity and nuances of flavor. One such coffee, from the Kirinyaga district of Kenya, is described as tasting like "malted grains and vanilla . . . almonds and orange brandy."

CONVERGENCE OF PAST AND PRESENT

Now Carlo Di Ruocco has passed the torch to his sons and daughter. As trends in the coffee world have come and gone, the family has tried to preserve Italian traditions without ignoring seismic shifts in the modern coffee industry. (You can get a sense of some of that history in a showroom attached to the Oakland roastery, which features beautifully restored espresso machines from the mid-twentieth century to the present.) In 2007 Di Ruocco's son

ROASTERY AND SHOWROOM:
696 3RD ST., OAKLAND

COFFEE BAR:
1890 BRYANT ST., SAN FRANCISCO

COFFEE BAR FiDi.
101 MONTGOMERY ST., SAN FRANCISCO

ROASTING SINCE
'82

5000–20,000 lb./week

on a Farina wood-fired roaster

FIND THE COFFEE AT MRESPRESSO.COM / COFFEE BAR

Luigi opened Coffee Bar, a contemporary café in the Mission (a second location opened in 2011). There, in a sleek, modern space amid the clacking of laptop keyboards, Mr. Espresso's coffees—both tradition-bound espresso and leading-edge single origins—are served up with great attention to detail by skilled baristas.

SCARLET CITY COFFEE ROASTING

IMPRESSIVE PEDIGREE, OLD-SCHOOL STYLE

In a basement on the campus of the University of California at Berkeley, Jen St. Hilaire stares at a zebra fish. She has managed this research facility for years—first to support her career in rock and roll, now to support her

> SCARLET CITY IS A DOUBLEPLUSGOOD ONE-WOMAN SHOW STARRING A SCI-FI-OBSESSED COFFEE VETERAN.

coffee-roasting habit. Yet St. Hilaire is no basement amateur: she has been roasting coffee since 1995. She roasted for Seattle's Espresso Vivace in the late 1990s and helped California's Ecco Caffe (now Ecco Roasting) get its start. In the Bay Area, a region now in love with bright, fruity, single-origin coffees, St. Hilaire offers an old-school counterpoint. The leather-clad roastmistress has chops, preferring and delivering sweet, balanced, medium-dark roasts and beautiful espresso blends.

INTRIGUING USE OF UNUSUAL INGREDIENTS

St. Hilaire knows what she likes: mouthfuls of chocolate. In her signature blends, Warp Drive and Light Speed, she aims to bring out both sweet and dark cocoa flavors and a maximum of velvety crema. To do this she uses an unusual recipe,

ROASTERY:
1304 WOOD ST.,
OAKLAND

ROASTING SINCE

'09

Less than 1000 lb./week

on a
Diedrich IR-12
roaster

FIND THE COFFEE AT
SCARLETCITYROASTING.COM
/ THEIR ROASTERY

including both Indian Monsooned Malabar and—sin of all sins—robusta beans. It is widely agreed that robusta coffee has a lower cup quality than arabica. St. Hilaire doesn't disagree, but she believes that in small quantities good robusta can stretch out the distinctive flavors in her blends, the same way a splash of water can bring out a good whiskey. Similarly, Malabars are unloved for being musty, but St. Hilaire finds they provide the perfect base for a full-bodied, sweet cup and produce a beautiful, deeply red-brown crema.

HIGHLIGHTING WOMEN IN THE INDUSTRY

Coffee has a reputation as a boys' club. Remarkably few coffee companies are owned by women, and just as few roasters are women. That's part of why St. Hilaire is proud to own Scarlet City and why she goes out of her way to find high-quality coffees from woman-owned farms and mills. One example is Epiphanie Mukashyaka. After losing her husband, child, and many other family members in the 1994 Rwandan genocide, Mukashyaka rebuilt the coffee farm she and her husband had owned, planting it with high-quality coffees. She also owns two coffee-washing stations where she employs local women. Her coffee has flavors of plum and honey and is showcased by Scarlet City as a single origin.

WOMEN IN COFFEE

Your favorite barista may be a member of the fairer sex, but in all likelihood your coffee roaster is not. The business of coffee has been dominated by men for about as long as it has been a global commodity (that's a couple hundred years). Nonetheless, the existence of high-quality coffee owes as much to women as it does to men. Erna Knutsen, a respected coffee trader since the 1970s, coined the term *specialty coffee*. Knutsen wasn't even allowed in the cupping room in her early days but eventually formed her own business and has been fueling change in the coffee industry ever since, supplying roasters like George Howell (formerly of The Coffee Connection) with some of the world's finest coffees. In the mid-1950s, Veda Younger at Boyd Coffee Company was the only female coffee buyer in America, and she remains one of only seven people to direct coffee purchasing in that company since its founding in 1900. A more recent pioneer is Karen Cebreros, founder in the early 1990s of Elan Organic Coffees, a specialty-coffee importer (now owned by InterAmerican Coffee) that worked extensively to support women farmers.

Now more than ever, women inhabit the back rooms of the coffee world, using their palates (which some scientists regard as more sensitive than men's) to taste, evaluate, roast, and source coffees. Many of today's most successful women in coffee hail from the Bay Area: Eileen Hassi, owner of Ritual Coffee Roasters; Helen Russell and Brooke McDonnell, owners of Equator Coffees & Teas; Trish Rothgeb, roaster and owner of Wrecking Ball Coffee Roasters; and Jen St. Hilaire, the one-woman-rock-act behind Scarlet City Coffee Roasting. For smaller, family-run outfits like Cellar Door and Extracto in Portland, husband-and-wife teams collaborate to keep the engines of business running.

Women do a substantial amount of the work on coffee farms, but few have ownership rights to the land they work. Cafe Femenino, an organization supporting women farmers, estimates that women make up 30 percent of all coffee growers and are responsible for producing 75 percent of the world's coffee. Yet women own less than 1 percent of the world's land. Nonprofits and aid agencies around the world fund projects to support women farmers, believing that women are generally more likely than men to reinvest in health, education, and community.

There is no clearinghouse for information about women-owned coffee companies or farms, but if you are interested in supporting women, start by looking at coffee roasters' websites. Many roasters provide information about the farms or co-ops where their coffee comes from and will mention if the owner is a woman or the co-op supports women farmers. Some companies, such as Portland Roasting and Equator Coffees & Teas, even invest in special projects to support women in coffee-growing communities. Cafe Femenino supplies woman-grown coffee to roasters around the U.S. from Peru, Colombia, and Mexico. Trailhead Coffee Roasters and Kobos Coffee both regularly carry their coffee.

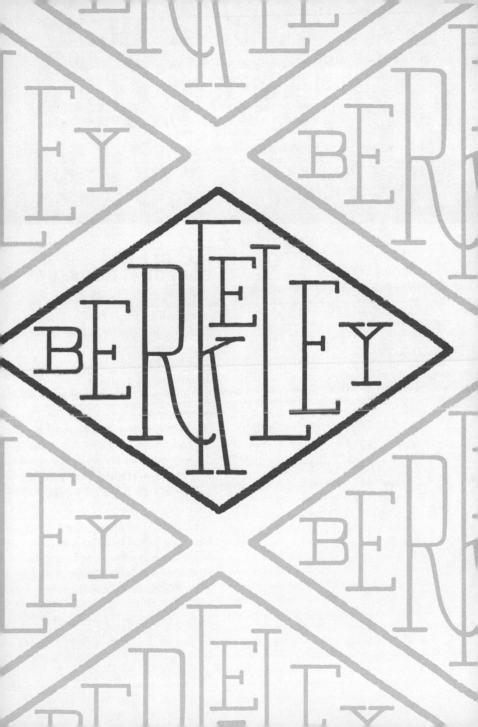

PEET'S COFFEE & TEA

IF YOU WANT TO TRACE WEST COAST COFFEE CULTURE AS WE KNOW IT BACK TO THE BEGINNING, YOU END UP AT THE CORNER OF WALNUT AND VINE IN BERKELEY.

PUT OFF BY CORPORATE COFFEE

In 1966 a young Dutch immigrant named Alfred Peet opened Peet's Coffee & Tea in Berkeley, selling coffee beans he had roasted by hand. Until then, San Francisco had been a coffee center of a different sort: a major port for green coffee (it still is), and a home base for megacompanies Folgers, Hills Brothers, and MJB, which together roasted millions of pounds of low-quality and instant coffee each year. Peet came onto the scene right as Big Coffee was getting bigger, with multinational buyouts by companies like Nestlé and Procter & Gamble. He was appalled by American coffee and wanted to offer something better. His father had been a coffee roaster in the Netherlands, and the young Alfred had worked for large coffee and tea importers. He knew where to get good coffee, and he knew how to roast it.

THE BEGINNING OF AN ERA

With Peet, the modern era of specialty coffee was born. His central innovations were the care he brought to sourcing coffee, his preference for blends, and his legendary dark roasting style, which continues to dominate in much of the country. He was among the first in the U.S. to import high-grown arabica coffees after World War II. The Berkeley café anchored a bustling neighborhood of food innovators, including the young Alice Waters of Chez Panisse, who focused as much attention on sourcing food as Peet did on coffee. Peet was on a crusade to educate and inspire—he is famous for his hours-long digressions on the beauty of the bean—and people paid attention. When the original Starbucks store opened in Seattle in 1971, it sold Peet's beans. When Starbucks' three founders began roasting their own, it was with Peet's instruction. Starbucks went on to popularize Peet's dark roasting style around the world, making it synonymous with West Coast coffee.

FLAGSHIP CAFÉ:
2124 VINE ST.,
BERKELEY

ROASTING SINCE

'66

More than 100,000 lb./week

on customized Probat roasters

FIND THE COFFEE AT PEETS.COM / THEIR NEARLY 200 CAFÉS NATIONWIDE

A LITTLE BIGGER BUT STILL HUMBLE

Alfred Peet sold Peet's Coffee & Tea in 1979, far earlier than most people realize given his central role in company legend. Nevertheless, Peet's has remained a relatively small, humble company in the scheme of things. Under the guidance of Jerry Baldwin, one of Starbucks' founders, Peet's grew from four stores to fifty-eight in 2000. Since the company went public in 2001, it has expanded to nearly two hundred stores, most of them in California, Oregon, and Washington (a mere fraction of the more than seventeen thousand stores Starbucks now operates). Even with a healthy brood of coffee bars, Peet's has never strayed far from its roots as a whole-bean slinger. The company still does a brisk mail-order business, shipping coffee to the homes of loyal Peetniks.

FORWARD LOOKING, IF NO LONGER LEADING

The original Peet's feels more like a regular café than the fountainhead of a movement, but a small back room does exhibit old photographs, menus, and ephemera, including the ceramic tasting cups Peet used to evaluate coffee from around the world. Though Peet died in 2007, the company keeps apace of major trends, like offering premium lots of single-origin coffees. Because of their decades-long relationships with growers, they have exclusive access to some high-quality and rare coffees. (Diehard Peetniks might want to spring for the $80-a-pound Jamaica Blue Mountain, though its reputation generally exceeds its performance.)

With sustainability initiatives on the ground in many coffee-growing regions, Peet's also strives to be a good corporate citizen. In 2007 the company opened the nation's first LEED Gold-certified roasting facility in Alameda, where they roast more than 100,000 pounds of coffee each week (and have room to roast more). Calling it small-batch roasting is a bit of a misnomer (batches are up to 600 pounds at once), but Peet's can still lay claim to the artisan nature of certain traditions—for example, their roasters must complete at least three years of training.

BAREFOOT COFFEE

SUNNY, AWARD-WINNING COFFEES

"It's hard to be pretentious when you don't have any shoes on." That's how Andy Newbom explains the name of the company he founded in 2003. (Nonetheless, the chef-turned-roaster-turned-coffee-buyer does appear to wear shoes most of the time himself.) Though Barefoot's original café sits smack in the middle of one of Silicon Valley's ubiquitous strip malls in Santa Clara, there's nothing pedestrian about their award-winning, small-batch coffees. In a surprisingly woodsy-posh space, Barefoot baristas dole out hand-poured, single-origin coffees and sprightly espressos, all roasted with a light touch to highlight California flavors—sunny, bright, and identifiably fruity.

BAREFOOT SERVES UP CHOCOLATE AND SUNSHINE IN THEIR AWARD-WINNING COFFEES FROM SIX COUNTRIES.

CONSISTENT TIES WITH FARMERS

Newbom took walking the coffee talk to a new level in 2011 by moving to El Salvador to live closer to coffee farms. For Barefoot, Newbom only buys coffee from El Salvador, Brazil, Costa Rica, Guatemala, and Ethiopia. The company is committed to the idea of relationship coffee, meaning they work with the same farmers year in, year out. This allows time for collaboration to improve the pruning, picking, and processing of the coffees, and provides a stable income for the farmers. In one example of the well-trod-path approach, Barefoot has purchased coffee from Edwin Martinez of Guatemala's Finca Vista Hermosa farm since 2005. The rela-tionship has led to special projects, like cordoning off areas of the farm to produce coffee exclusively for Barefoot.

THE BOSS IS IN CHARGE

Barefoot's house espresso, The Boss, is a chocolate bomb. The fudginess comes from Redcab, a special blend within the blend, a mix of Brazilian varietals that Newbom developed in conjunction with his partners at Daterra Farms. The other ingredients in The Boss can bring in flavors as wide-ranging as butterscotch and anise; since the blend changes three times a year, you'll want try it often. Barefoot also offers rotating seasonal blends created from the same estates whose coffees are sold as single origins. All the roasting happens in San Jose. If you make the trek to one of the South Bay Area cafés, order two cups: whatever you want to start, and a cappuccino made with The Boss for dessert.

ROASTERY:
76 SUNOL ST.,
SAN JOSE

FLAGSHIP CAFÉ:
5237 STEVENS
CREEK BLVD.,
SANTA CLARA

ROASTING SINCE

'03

1000-5000 lb./week

on Probat L12 and Diedrich IR-24 roasters

FIND THE COFFEE AT BAREFOOTCOFFEE.COM / THEIR ROASTERY / THEIR SOUTH BAY AREA CAFÉS

SAN
RAFAEL

EQUATOR COFFEES & TEAS

GOOD COFFEE ON THE FLY

After sixteen years of business, Equator Coffees & Teas finally opened its first retail showcase café in an unlikely place—the San Francisco International Airport. Owners Helen Russell and Brooke McDonnell originally ran the company out of a garage; now their state-of-the-art roasting works is in San Rafael. The café is part of a regional food court in SFO's Terminal 2 (by the same developer who created the famed Ferry Building Marketplace). With a pour-over bar for slow-coffee geeks and iced blended drinks for the uninitiated, it offers travelers a to-go taste of San Francisco's coffee scene, without a lot of fuss.

THEIR OWN FLEDGLING FARM

A trip from SFO to the airport in David, Panama, requires four flights and takes up to twenty-eight hours, but

EQUATOR COFFEES & TEAS CATERS TO THE JET SET.

from there it's a short drive to Cerro Punta. Here, a mere 8 degrees north of the equator and 7000 feet above sea level, sits Equator's farm, Finca Sophia. After purchasing it in 2008 with coffee legend Willem Boot, Equator planted twenty-five thousand trees of the exalted Geisha varietal, which began to bear their first crop in 2011. Geisha coffees are famous for their sweet, clean character and honey-citrus flavor with a bergamot burnish. Equator's goal: to dig in—literally—to what it means to produce sustainable, high-quality coffee from seed to cup. Finca Sophia is perhaps the most extreme example of the company's tendency to kick up dirt. They also run a microloan program for farms to upgrade their processing equipment, roast on a low-energy-consumption roaster, and have trained farmers in Africa to reuse coffee pulp waste for growing food.

SPECIAL BLENDS FOR LEGENDARY CHEFS

For its commitment to sustainability, Equator has earned a following among the food world's glitterati. Thomas Keller, chef at the highly regarded French Laundry, first encountered the coffee at a café near his famous Napa eatery. Ever since, Equator has provided special blends for Keller and other celebrity chefs, like Traci Des Jardins and Iron Chef Masaharu Morimoto. Their coffee is available in many high-end restaurants from Napa to New York. But you don't have to leave home to enjoy them—some of these chef blends can be purchased through the website.

CAFÉ:
NAPA FARMS MARKET, TERMINAL 2 SAN FRANCISCO AIRPORT

ROASTING SINCE
'95

5000–20,000 lb./week

on Loring and Petroncini Impianti roasters

FIND THE COFFEE AT EQUATORCOFFEES.COM / THEIR CAFÉ

WEAVER'S COFFEE & TEA

APPRENTICE TO THE MASTERS

John Weaver was the master roaster at Peet's Coffee & Tea for more than twenty years, making him one of the most experienced roasters in the business. He began work at Peet's as a delivery boy at age twenty. Alfred Peet took him under his wing, and Weaver found himself apprenticing under two renowned coffee experts, Peet and Sal Bonavita (who bought Peet's in 1979). One of the first lessons Peet taught him? Don't snort cocaine. Don't snort *anything*. (Snorting deadens the palate, a critical tool for any roaster.) Weaver also learned to keep his opinions to himself at the tasting table unless asked to speak, an education which served him well for his long career at Peet's. In 2007 Weaver got the itch to start something new. Weaver's Coffee & Tea was born of his desire to return to roasting small batches and to develop his own blends.

A ROAST TO SINK YOUR TEETH INTO

Weaver roasts coffee on a 45-kilo Probat, which he calls the Stradivarius of roasting machines, carrying on the dark-roasting tradition he learned at Peet's. He wants you to taste the pungent caramel sweetness of the roasting process itself. If you can't taste the roast, Weaver says, he hasn't done his job. His style is juicy, with huge body—these coffees bloom in your mouth. A chart on the website rating each coffee's level of roast, flavor complexity, body, and acidity makes it easy to choose between a dark-roasted, low-acidity French roast, for example, and a high-acidity, low-body Africa blend.

Weaver's uses a vintage
Royal No. 5 to create a
special blend of coffee in
honor of Alfred Peet.

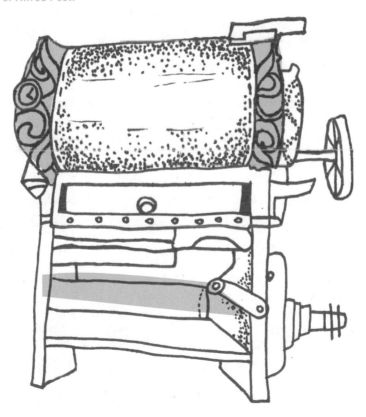

Weaver's carries a few "1-origin" coffees, identified by country and region, but that's as close as the roaster gets to third-wave coffee. In keeping with the old-school politics of the industry and the belief that mystery is important, John Weaver doesn't divulge the contents of his blends, the names of the farms he buys from, or the specifics of his roast style—ironclad rules he learned from Peet himself.

PEET'S VETERAN ROASTER JOHN WEAVER STRIKES OUT ON HIS OWN BUT KEEPS A LEGACY ALIVE.

HOMAGE TO PEET AND BONAVITA

June through September, Weaver unearths an ancient relic of a roasting machine. The stubbornly beautiful Royal No. 5—curlicued with brass, like something from a vintage carnival display—was built in 1905. On it, Weaver roasts a special Legacy Blend in honor of Peet and Bonavita, 15 pounds at a time (which he then blends with coffee roasted on the Probat). The blend has a smoky flavor, owing to the fact that flames actually touch the beans, burning chaff and creating smoke. When Peet himself began roasting at his first store in San Francisco, he used another 1905 Royal, making it the machine on which a movement was born. Weaver bought the original in 2008 and keeps it on proud display in his roastery and tasting room.

ROASTERY AND TASTING ROOM:
40 LOUISE STREET, SAN RAFAEL

ROASTING SINCE
'07

5000-20,000 lb./week

on a 45-kilo Probat roaster

FIND THE COFFEE AT WEAVERSCOFFEE.COM / TASTING ROOM

ROASTMASTER IN ACTION

The roastery, which is open to the public, sits in the shadow of a Highway 101 overpass in San Rafael. The attached tasting room feels a bit like a spare, modern bachelor pad, with black leather chairs, wide flatscreen TV, animal-print rug, and seafoam green walls. Look past the barista to a big picture window and you'll see John Weaver doing what he loves—roasting coffee on his Probat, one batch at a time.

FLYING GOAT COFFEE

LIGHTER ROASTS IN SMALLER CUPS

When Flying Goat first opened in 1994, it was a different kind of coffee company, and Healdsburg was a different kind of town. The town was sleepy, and true to the 1990s, Flying Goat's coffee was dark-roasted and presented in giant cups. Over the next decade, as Healdsburg transformed into an international wine destination, coffee culture lagged. But in 2007, Flying Goat owners Phil Anacker and Maura Harrington decided to change everything: ditch the 16-ounce paper cups, forswear dark roasting, and focus on buying stellar small lots of single-origin coffees. The goal: to showcase coffee as complex and elegant as any wine.

SOMETHING TO SAVOR

Flying Goat is surrounded by people with deeply educated palates—wine drinkers—who embrace the similarities between coffee and their beverage of choice. The idea of *terroir* is well established in wine. Visitors to Flying Goat's chic, rustic-industrial café on Healdsburg's town square are quick to catch on to the similarities, such as how picking the ripest fruit and carefully sorting it translates into better quality in the cup. But unlike wine, which is hard to ruin once bottled, good coffee is terrifically easy to

IN THE
HEART OF WINE
COUNTRY,
A COFFEE COMPANY
BRINGS
TERROIR TO LIFE.

mutilate—during the milling process, by roasting it too light or too dark, by using dirty brewing equipment, or by over- or underextracting the grounds. Accordingly, Anacker encourages customers to savor a beautiful coffee as a minor miracle.

BLIND TASTINGS THAT PROVE A POINT

If you ask the folks at Flying Goat for dark-roasted coffee, they'll set up a blind tasting of your favorite dark coffee alongside one of their more lightly roasted ones. Baristas have done this dozens of times, and Anacker reports that a single customer has yet to pick the dark-roasted coffee. The contents of the medium-roasted house espresso blend, Espresso No. 9, change four or five times a year based on the harvest seasons. It's a treat in a latte, but you may have more fun trying out your wine vocabulary on one of Flying Goat's single-origin offerings. Is it unctuous or brawny or chewy? Big or buttery? When you're done, head across the square and reward yourself with a magnum of the hard stuff at one of dozens of wineries in town.

ROASTERY AND TASTING ROOM: 419 CENTER ST., HEALDSBURG

ROASTING SINCE '94

ORIGINAL CAFÉ: 324 CENTER STREET, HEALDSBURG

1000-5000 lb./week

on Probat UG22, L5 roasters

FIND THE COFFEE AT FLYINGGOATCOFFEE.COM / THEIR TASTING ROOM / HEALDSBURG AND SANTA ROSA CAFÉS

SANTA CRUZ

VERVE COFFEE ROASTERS

PRECISE COFFEE IN A SLEEK SPACE

You can see the ocean from the doorstep of Verve's original café and roastery. It's a stone's throw from a popular surfing beach at the north end of Monterey Bay. But don't mistake Verve for some sleepy beach operation catering to sunburned tourists. In the café you'll find a black walnut and concrete bar, sleek cocoa-colored leather benches, and a coterie of play-hard-work-harder baristas. From the rotating single-origin espressos, to the meticulous latte art, to the roasting operations on full display, Verve dispenses with any notion that a laid-back lifestyle should include slouchy coffee. A second roastery (with walk-up coffee bar) and a café in downtown Santa Cruz exude the same breezy confidence.

FINDING THAT SWEET SPOT

Verve carries a dozen carefully sourced, seasonal single origins at any time, from the papaya-and-hibiscus La Montañita (El Salvador) to the maple-and-spice Los Naranjos (Colombia). The biscuity, chocolaty Sermon espresso blend is more or less the same year-round and is as close as Verve comes to a traditional coffee. The Streetlevel espresso blend, by contrast, is a platform for experimentation. Featuring a selection of single varietal and estate coffees from Latin America, the mix changes at least

> DESPITE BEING IN A LAID-BACK BEACH TOWN, VERVE HAS VIM AND VIGOR.

three times a year as new coffees come into season. On one visit it might taste like champagne, honey, and oranges (with coffee from Brazil and El Salvador); swap in a Caturra varietal from Guatemala, and the chocolate volume rises to eleven. Verve has earned a reputation for roasting coffee right to its sweet spot, whether it's a delicate Papua New Guinea or a burly Brazil.

ORIGINAL ROASTERY & CAFÉ: 816 41ST AVE., SANTA CRUZ

SEABRIGHT ROASTERY & COFFEE BAR: 104 BRONSON ST., SUITE 19, SANTA CRUZ

ROASTING SINCE '07

1000-5000 lb./week

on Probat L12, G45 roasters

FIND THE COFFEE AT VERVECOFFEE ROASTERS.COM / THEIR ROASTERIES & CAFÉS

COFFEE, KEYBOARDS, AND MAPPING SKILLS

Colby Barr, Verve's cofounder and green buyer, came to coffee slantwise. He grew up a farmer's son, then spent years mapping disaster areas for FEMA. A shared love of vintage Fender Rhodes keyboards brought him together with Chico State classmate and coffee fanatic Ryan O'Donovan. Since the two founded Verve, Barr's background in mapping has come in handy, helping them understand why certain geographical variables affect flavor. Knowing that the hills of a steep, narrow valley in El Salvador produced a recent favorite, Barr might visit farms in a similar microclimate in Costa Rica to look for new possibilities.

SACRAMENTO

TEMPLE COFFEE

COMFY, FRIENDLY, POPULAR

If you're heading to a Temple café on a weekend morning, go early. Coffee culture has thrived for decades in the Bay Area, but great, locally roasted beans have only recently made their way to the dry interior valley. Temple began roasting its own coffee in 2010 after five years as one of the city's most notable cafés. The roastery and flagship café is warm and comfy, with lots of exposed wood and brick, and deep leather couches (a touch rarely found in the hoity-toity coffee world). A slick downtown café is more spare. No matter where you go, the baristas are knowledgeable and welcoming, letting you know the name of the farm for each coffee you order, without being pushy.

BARISTA SMACKDOWN

Despite the peaceful aura at Temple, many of their baristas take their love

ROASTERY AND FLAGSHIP CAFÉ:
2829 S ST., SACRAMENTO

DOWNTOWN CAFÉ:
1010 9TH ST., SACRAMENTO

ROASTING SINCE
'10

1000-5000 lb./week

on Probat UG15 and Probatino roasters

FIND THE COFFEE AT TEMPLECOFFEE.COM / THEIR CAFÉS

of coffee to the mat in the rarefied world of barista competitions. On stage, coffee slingers duke it out in front of hundreds of onlookers, each preparing three drinks for seven judges—an espresso, a cappuccino, and a signature drink. They may spend up to eight months ahead of time working with Temple's roastmaster to build a custom blend for competition. Glory doesn't come cheap, however. Giving competitors what they need to prepare—namely green coffee, milk, and everyone's time—can cost thousands of dollars. Sean Kohmescher, Temple's owner and a former competition barista himself, is happy to make the investment. Competitions help professionalize the work and, more importantly, showcase Temple's coffees to the industry's biggest evangelists.

IN DRY, SUNNY SACRAMENTO, A GOOD PLACE FOR COFFEE WORSHIP CAN BE HARD TO FIND.

ARTFUL Q-CERTIFIED ROASTING

The high priests of coffee are Q (quality) graders, who have put their knowledge and palates to the test in a rigorous certification process. Approximately thirteen hundred of them exist. Their monastic-sounding code of ethics states, among other things, "Be honest with the coffee," and "Follow the rule of silent work." Temple's Ed Whitman is a rare specimen: a Q-certified roaster. His expertise allows him to trace the finest nuances of flavor and aroma—including defects, like the slight moldy blueberry taste of overfermented coffee. He uses his skills to decide which coffees to buy, carefully craft roasts for the dozen or so single origins on the menu at any given time, and regularly tweak the house espresso, Dharma Blend. All this voodoo adds up to a coffee experience in California's central desert that is worth a pilgrimage.

THANKSGIVING COFFEE COMPANY

COFFEE'S GONZO CONSCIENCE

Thanksgiving's story is impossible to separate from the story of its founder, Paul Katzeff. Abrasive and brazen, he once declared himself "God's gift to coffee." But he has done as much as anyone to push the idea that quality in the cup and quality of life on the farm are inextricably linked. Katzeff is a provocateur of the first order: he was Hunter S. Thompson's campaign manager in 1970 during Thompson's bid to become sheriff of Pitkin County, Colorado, under the Freak Power ticket; he sued the Reagan White House in 1985 over a trade embargo with Nicaragua, then defied the embargo by importing coffee through Canada; and in 1990 he dumped buckets of fake blood on the steps of a hotel where coffee professionals were meeting, to encourage a boycott of "death squad coffee" from El Salvador. His provocations are

ROASTERY AND TASTING ROOM:
19100 S HARBOR DR., FORT BRAGG

ROASTING SINCE

'72

5000-20,000 lb./week

on a 60-kilo G. W. Barth roaster

FIND THE COFFEE AT THANKSGIVINGCOFFEE.COM / THEIR ROASTERY

matched by a serious argument that social justice and gourmet coffee are mutually inclusive.

FIRST CUPPING LABS FOR FARMERS

During a trip to Nicaragua in 1996, Katzeff asked a group of coffee farmers if they had ever tasted their own coffee. Only one hand went up. The next year, Thanksgiving secured a $405,000 grant from USAID to build nine innovative cupping labs in Nicaragua. Once farmers had the tools to evaluate quality themselves, they could both demand appropriate compensation and adjust their practices to produce better coffees. It was such a good idea that the practice of farmers and buyers tasting coffee together has become a staple for quality-focused coffee roasters. Byron Corrales, a Nicaraguan farmer who planted his first coffee tree at age seven, codirected the cupping lab project. He went on to produce a special varietal called Maracaturra, a cross of Maragogipe and Caturra; it has twice scored an exceptional 94 points from coffeereview.com, which describes it as having "hints of dusk-blooming flowers and chocolate."

FOCUSED ON COOPERATIVES

Though Katzeff has retired, the company's motto remains "Not just a cup, but a just cup." Thanksgiving is dedicated to working with cooperatives, believing it's where they can have the greatest impact on farmer quality of life (many estate coffee farms are owned by relatively wealthy individuals or families, whereas cooperatives provide infrastructure for small, generally poor farmers). One cooperative was formed in Uganda in 2004 by an interfaith group of Muslim, Christian, and Jewish farmers who wanted to get better prices for their coffees and promote collaboration. They call their coffee Mirembe Kawomera, or Delicious Peace. Thanksgiving bought the entire crop, 37,500 pounds, in 2004, the first year of their relationship with the co-op. By 2011 the farmers were producing 112,500 pounds of coffee, more than Thanksgiving could buy. Thanksgiving sells Delicious Peace at a discount to churches, synagogues, and mosques in the U.S. The coffee comes in both light- and dark-roasted versions; the pecan and chocolate notes in the light roast turn smoky and caramelized in the dark. In other projects, Thanksgiving—among the first to embrace Fair Trade and to criticize its faltering direction—focuses on the problems farmers will face in coming decades, especially business development and climate change.

FROM A REMOTE TOWN HALFWAY BETWEEN SAN FRANCISCO AND THE OREGON BORDER, A LITTLE-KNOWN, VISIONARY COFFEE COMPANY INFLUENCED THE ENTIRE COFFEE INDUSTRY.

TELLING THE GROWERS' STORIES

Thanksgiving's gorgeous website features some of the most well-thought-out, engaging portraits of coffee farmers out there. (Though it's trendy to profile farms and farmers, few companies do a great job of it.) The content is peppered with contributions by farmers themselves, halted English and all. Thanksgiving's coffees are hard to find outside of northern California but can be ordered online. They tend to be medium to dark in their roast, but some single origins are roasted more lightly to preserve origin character. Call ahead for a tour at their roastery. Though Katzeff has retired, his quirks, energy, and idealism still animate the business. On LinkedIn, his interests are listed as "baseball, mushrooms, coffee, marijuana cultivation and use issues, sustainability applications in business, antique Patagonian side trays (pre-Colombian)."

WRECKING BALL COFFEE ROASTERS

With the mighty swing of not one but two veteran coffee pros from the East Coast, Wrecking Ball Coffee Roasters is bulldozing a trail through the San Francisco coffee world. Trish Rothgeb, roastmaster, green coffee buyer, and certified Q grader, has been in the coffee business since 1986 and is credited with coining the term *third wave* to describe the emergence of coffee's hyper-quality movement. Nicholas Cho, her partner, is an opinionated career barista with a passion for making high-end specialty coffee more accessible to the public. The dynamic duo, based in Palo Alto, strives to be "the area's most recognized purveyor of sustainably sourced, expertly roasted specialty coffee." They are also customer-focused in an era of indifferent hipsterism. That doesn't mean they'll serve you a raspberry latte; it just means they'll be really nice about not serving you a raspberry latte. Find out more at wreckingballcoffee.com.

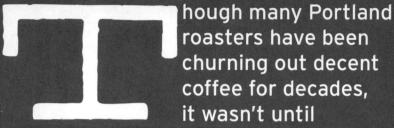

Though many Portland roasters have been churning out decent coffee for decades, it wasn't until Stumptown Coffee Roasters opened in 1999 that the coffee landscape began to take on its present-day contours. By 2005 a flood of microroasters were opening shop and garnering the attention of the coffee world at large.

Many of Portland's newer roasters taught themselves to roast and have a touch of the city's DIY, fly-by-the-seat-of-your-pants attitude about them. The approach seems to work in a town where consumers are willing to take a chance on small, mom-and-pop businesses. The city is notable for the sheer number of small roasting outfits and the nuanced variety of approaches, from traditional Italian recipes for espresso to extremely light-roasted, Scandinavian-style coffee.

Almost every neighborhood in central
Portland has its own small roaster.
Portlanders have embraced single
origins, cheerfully consuming stories
about farms and co-ops along with
their coffee.

Quality coffee has a firm foothold
in a few population centers outside of
Portland—in the central, high-desert city
of Bend, for example, or the southern
valley town of Ashland. (College
towns Eugene and Corvallis, and the
state capital, Salem, are significant
exceptions; students and legislators
have to make do with middling brew.)
Coffee has yet to reach the status
of craft beer in Oregon, where even
the diviest bars offer a selection of
stellar local brews, but great beans are
relatively easy to find in the primary
and secondary cities if you know where
to look.

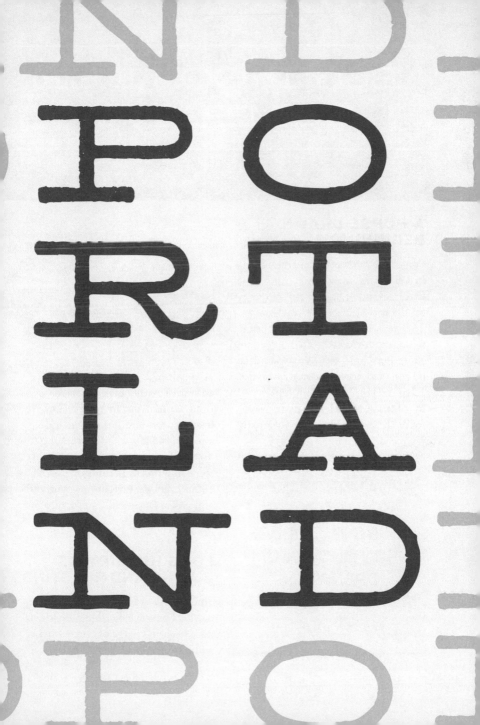

PORTLAND

BOYD COFFEE COMPANY

A HORSE-DRAWN BEGINNING

Forget the sizzle of the steam wand—in 1900, you knew it was coffee time by the sound of hooves clip-clopping on the street in front of your house. That year, Percival Dewe Boyd began selling fresh-roasted coffee, spices, and tea to Portland's expanding populace out of a red horse-drawn wagon. By 1910 the horses had been replaced by a fleet of Model Ts. Fast-forward to 1971, and Boyd Coffee Company,

or Boyds, was a fully modern coffee enterprise with a brand-new 30-acre headquarters outside of Portland. The headquarters is still there, including a roastery and warehouse totaling 400,000 square feet. From it, Boyds ships millions of pounds of roasted coffee every year to cafés, restaurants, and grocery stores as far as Chicago and Texas.

> ROASTING SINCE 1900, BOYDS IS AMONG THE OLDEST CONTINUOUSLY OPERATING ROASTERS ON THE WEST COAST.

LONG HISTORY OF BUYING AND ROASTING

Since Boyds was founded, only six remarkably knowledgeable individuals have been in charge of coffee buying and roasting. P. D.'s great-grandson

A fleet of carriages and Model Ts once delivered Boyds coffee to customers' homes.

Michael is apprenticing to be the seventh buyer-roaster, a process that will take close to a decade and involve many thousands of slurps of coffee. In the 1950s Boyds promoted Veda Younger to the position, making her the controversial first female green coffee buyer in America. These days the company roasts all of its coffees—thirty blends and three single origins, plus decaf, in medium to dark roasts—on four car-sized, cast-iron drum roasters. They are connected to a vast computer system that moves the coffee through silos and tubes in its evolution from green, to roasted, to ground, to packaged and shipped. Like most roasters of the company's size, Boyds purchases coffee by the container load (37,500 pounds each). Uniquely, Boyds imports most of its coffee directly into the Port of Portland. The company has worked with many of its farm partners for decades, and signs contracts with trusted sources as much as a year before the harvest. Most of the coffees, from all major growing regions, are combined into blends, many of which have been around for decades (at one time there were as many as eighty blends). The Gourmet Medallion is as close to a signature blend as Boyds gets—a balanced, medium-roasted drip coffee from Central America and East Africa.

BRINGING IT ALL UP TO DATE

Boyds remains in the family. In 2010 the third generation retired and passed the baton to the fourth. Among the first orders of business? Replacing the chairs and tables that have been sitting in the Boyds lobby since the 1970s. A much harder task will be updating the company's image. Due to its longevity, Boyds has weathered global spikes and steep crashes in coffee prices, as well as changing tastes. It has kept up with the times partly by making convenience items like powdered drinks, espresso pods, and even gravy bases. In recent years, Boyds has consistently focused on innovative brewing technology. It was the first company to import the Swedish-made Technivorm Moccamaster in the 1980s—still undisputedly the best automated home drip machine available. But attitudes toward coffee have changed significantly over the years, and the new generation's task is to translate Boyds' success in the last century into success in this one. Case

in point: attached to the roastery, in a far-out industrial zone of Portland, is a knick-knacky store and café where you can taste most Boyds coffees in an atmosphere that is très 1973. For a slightly updated experience, find the company's mobile coffee cart at a festival or park around town.

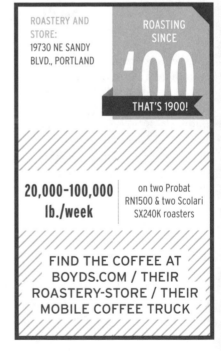

ROASTERY AND STORE:
19730 NE SANDY BLVD., PORTLAND

ROASTING SINCE

'00

THAT'S 1900!

20,000-100,000 lb./week

on two Probat RN1500 & two Scolari SX240K roasters

FIND THE COFFEE AT BOYDS.COM / THEIR ROASTERY-STORE / THEIR MOBILE COFFEE TRUCK

CELLAR DOOR COFFEE ROASTERS

GETTING STARTED AT FARMERS' MARKETS

Andrea Pastor loves the focus and physicality of roasting coffee, which she considers a delightfully arcane profession. One of the few female coffee roasters in Portland, Pastor refined her approach by selling beans at local farmers' markets, where customers could taste different coffees side by side and share their observations. Puddletown, the house blend for espresso and drip, is a medium-roasted mix (usually) of Peruvian, Guatemalan, and Ethiopian coffees—mildly chocolaty with a bright note. Cellar Door's baristas are instrumental in giving feedback on the blend and on a changing selection of single origins, which fits perfectly with the familial feel of the bright corner shop. Adding to the atmosphere are Pastor's perpetually smiling parents, who help run the business (because, Pastor quips, she can't get anyone else to work for cappuccinos).

> CELLAR DOOR EPITOMIZES A MOM-AND-POP APPROACH THAT PORTLAND COFFEE CULTURE IS KNOWN FOR.

A GREENER CUP (AND OTHER INNOVATIONS)

While Pastor stokes the fire, husband Jeremy Adams chats up customers, trains baristas, and—his favorite pastime of all—tinkers with the shop's machinery. Adams custom-built a system to clean the smoke generated by roasting using misted water (it's greener and cheaper than factory-made alternatives). His bookshelf is packed with monographs on topics like the physics of boomerangs, ducting air flow, and how to grow nut trees. He and Pastor have been working on a plan to drastically decrease the number of paper cups thrown out in coffee-crazy Portland through a city-wide reusable cup scheme.

IN PURSUIT OF ETHICAL COFFEES

Pastor and Adams have been on board with the organic and Fair Trade movement since the beginning. They are committed to preserving natural resources and helping coffee growers achieve viable economic futures. But they acknowledge that certifications alone will not accomplish this—the Fair Trade organization in particular hasn't kept pace with changes in the coffee industry. Consequently, they continue to carry certified coffees but also offer coffees that they know to be grown sustainably and with appropriate working conditions. The couple's travels through coffee-growing regions have reinforced their views about the complexity of the global coffee trade. They work hard to be ethical in their purchases, knowing they'll never have all the answers.

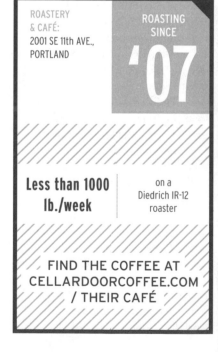

ROASTERY & CAFÉ:
2001 SE 11th AVE., PORTLAND

ROASTING SINCE
'07

Less than 1000 lb./week

on a Diedrich IR-12 roaster

FIND THE COFFEE AT CELLARDOORCOFFEE.COM / THEIR CAFÉ

NECTAR COFFEE COMPANY

With wife, son, four chickens, and cat in tow, Todd Weiler packed up his life in Healdsburg, California, where he roasted for Flying Goat Coffee, and moved to Portland. He quickly set up shop as a tiny one-man show, using an Ambex YM-2 (2-kilo) machine to roast a small selection of sustainably grown single-origin coffees. Nectar's beginnings in Portland were humble, with a small online shop and a regular Sunday booth at a suburban farmers' market (slinging both bags of whole-bean coffee and hot cups to go, made by hand). But considering Weiler's background roasting for Flying Goat and Chicago's Intelligentsia, Nectar is sure to sweeten Portland's roasting scene for the foreseeable future. Find out more at nectarcoffeecompany.com.

CLIVE COFFEE

WELL-MADE, HEAVY ON SEX APPEAL

Clive Coffee is an online company presenting a totally curated experience for the coffee nerd at home. To begin with, they sell only a small selection of the best equipment available for home preparation—everything from Rancilio single-group espresso machines, to elegant Frieling stainless-steel French presses, to sleek Stelton carafes. They don't overwhelm you with options, offering only well-made, durable gear that's heavy on sex appeal. Everything is drool-worthy, including their own small-batch coffees. Through the website, Clive brings Portland-style, medium-roasted, single-origin coffees to home baristas across the country. At their showroom in Portland, built on the Apple Store see-for-yourself model, you can take a class on how to use equipment properly, and get a chance to stroke and cuddle (and, yes, pull and steam) some of the most beautifully designed instruments of the trade.

NEXUS OF DESIGN AND COFFEE

Owner Mark Hellweg loves well-designed, ritual-forward objects that contribute to the aesthetic dimension of coffee making and drinking—particularly when they reflect the artisan status of his favorite coffees (his own included). With that in mind, he has

> CLIVE COFFEE BRINGS THE BEST IN COFFEE PORN— GEEKY GADGETS, SVELTE MACHINES— RIGHT INTO YOUR HOME.

commissioned local woodworkers and ceramicists to design handmade items for the kitchen counter. One such item is a curved pour-over stand for single cups of coffee (made of warm-toned Oregon walnut salvaged from the bottom of the Willamette River), which fits a jaunty, white pour-over cone and mug set created by Pigeon Toe Ceramics.

THE PRACTICAL SIDE OF BEAUTY

Everything Clive does is in the service of demystifying great coffee for home baristas, many of whom are scattered far from urban centers of coffee culture. Detailed how-to guides and videos cover everything from making a decent French press to how to drain an espresso machine boiler. Clive's own small menu of single-origin beans offers a more subtle kind of education. Four simple flavor groups—sweet, balanced; fruity, floral; chocolaty, nutty; and smoky,

SHOWROOM:
79 SE TAYLOR ST.,
PORTLAND

ROASTING SINCE

'08

Less than 1000 lb./week

on a 6-kilo Probat roaster

FIND THE COFFEE AT CLIVECOFFEE.COM / THEIR SHOWROOM

robust—help customers explore similarities and differences among origins. A changing menu reinforces the basic lesson that coffee changes seasonally. The sole year-round espresso blend, Lovejoy, is fruity but plays well with milk—it's geared to be perfect in a macchiato, the aha! drink that helps newer home baristas discover the joys of espresso.

COAVA COFFEE ROASTERS

★

ONE-OFF FLAVOR AND EXCLUSIVITY

Visiting Coava's website gives you a sense of just how seriously they take coffee. Open up a screen of their carefully curated single-origin lineup, and you'll find out where and who the farmer is, how many natural springs (or kids!) cross the property, and what kind of taste notes will eventually grace your palate. For the company's two founders, best friends Matt Higgins and Keith Gehrke, it's all about flavor—the more unusual or complex the better—and exclusivity. Higgins roasts only estate and microlot coffees, and when he likes something, he buys up the entire production run, ensuring that coffee you get from Coava is unlikely to be available anywhere else in the world. Especially favored are beans whose lead note is fruity (coffee, Higgins likes to point out, starts as a cherry). The Honduras El Limon, for one, tastes like a sweet-tart pineapple upside-down cake.

CLEAN LINES AND A PAPER CUP (IF YOU ASK NICELY)

Coava's airy, open tasting room perfectly reflects the marriage of technology, art, and sustainability that defines the business. Most everything but the roasting machine, which sits in plain view, is made of clean-lined bamboo (the café doubles as the showroom for Bamboo Revolution, a design company). The cabinetry literally glows, soaring all the way to the ceiling, and tables are fashioned from salvaged industrial machinery. At the minimalist bar, one of Coava's award-winning baristas presents you with an equally minimalist choice of two coffees and two methods of preparation: you can have drip coffee manually brewed in a Chemex, or a ristretto (short) shot of espresso, plain or in a macchiato, cappuccino, or small latte. Milk, sugar, and paper cups are kept behind the bar—out of sight, out of mind. High art prevails

COAVA SOURCES MICROLOT BEANS FROM AROUND THE WORLD, ROASTS THEM WITH A FANATICAL ATTENTION TO DETAIL, THEN BREWS THEM WITH EQUIPMENT THEY DESIGNED THEMSELVES. NERDS.

at Coava. The purist atmosphere may put off casual coffee enthusiasts, but it shouldn't. The coffee is too good.

EXACTING, NOT TO SAY OBSESSIVE

As proof of the level of their obsession, Gehrke has also started Able Brewing Equipment, a company that makes, among other things, the Kone, a reusable metal coffee filter used in Chemex brewers. The Kone has earned points for sustainability and its effect on flavor and body: yummy oils but little sediment pass through the filter. Need further proof? Higgins's latest project is growing hundreds of coffee plants in his Portland basement. The purpose isn't to harvest the coffee but to understand how coffee grows. He believes it will help him become a smarter buyer of coffee and give the company an edge in sourcing novel, beautiful beans. Coava's exacting, not to say obsessive standards at every level have earned it its place among premier small roasters in the United States—a success due in large

part to the thriving coffee culture of Portland, where coffee lovers aren't put off by limited menus and coffee that tastes, for example, like "black tea, lemonade, and anise" (the Ethiopia Kochere).

ROASTERY AND CAFÉ:
1300 SE GRAND AVE., PORTLAND

ROASTING SINCE
'09

1000-5000 lb./week

on a Probat L5 roaster

FIND THE COFFEE AT COAVA.MYSHOPIFY.COM / THEIR CAFÉ

COFFEE BEAN INTERNATIONAL & PUBLIC DOMAIN

BIGGER DOESN'T ALWAYS MEAN BADDER

CBI roasts 19 million pounds of coffee a year, making it one of the largest specialty roasters in the country. Insiders primarily know it as a private label roaster that provides coffee for Nordstrom, Target, and other well-known businesses. The company largely flew under the public's radar until 2010, when it opened Public Domain, a flagship café in downtown Portland. CBI and Public Domain invert the commonplace idea that bigger equals badder. Though only about 5 percent of CBI's coffee meets the highest standards of quality, the green buying team spends up to half its time finding and perfecting these gems, which are sold at Public Domain. The café is also among the few places to get great coffee in Portland's downtown core.

ROASTERY AND TASTING ROOM:
9120 NE ALDERWOOD RD., PORTLAND

PUBLIC DOMAIN:
603 SW BROADWAY AVE., PORTLAND

PUBLIC DOMAIN ROASTING SINCE
'10

Less than 1000 lb./week

on 1-kilo, 45-kilo Probat roasters

FIND THE COFFEE AT THEIR TASTING ROOM / PUBLIC DOMAIN

GROUNDBREAKING WORK WITH FARMERS

In the late 1980s, green coffee buyer and roaster Paul Thornton began traveling regularly to coffee farms. He quickly realized that many of the so-so coffees he encountered had the potential to be great. Most coffee at the time was a hodgepodge of mediocre beans and excellent beans that had been mixed together before exportation. Since he worked directly with farmers, Thornton could identify the great coffees and ask that they be held aside (for a premium, of course). This practice, though now common, put Thornton and CBI at the forefront of a radical change in the specialty-coffee world.

DELVE INTO AN EVOLVING BLEND

Despite its corporate provenance, Public Domain keeps pace with the best independent cafés in Portland. The café is clean and modern, stripped bare of extraneous detail to keep the attention on the coffee. You can choose from a deep menu of single origins, prepared while you wait

COFFEE BEAN INTERNATIONAL IS A GIANT AMONG WEST COAST ROASTERS, BUT YOU'VE LIKELY NEVER HEARD OF THEM.

at a pour-over bar, by French press, or as espresso. The house blend, Prometheus, is an evolving creature, constantly reborn with the freshest green coffee available. Customers are encouraged to explore the blend as it changes—it may have a particular fruit-centered sweetness one month, a buttery texture the next. CBI roasts the coffee for Public Domain separately from their large clients' beans. Why go to the effort? It gives them a chance to showcase the approach to coffee they believe in most.

THE LITTLEST ROASTERS

Coffee is big business. The U.S. imported nearly 3 billion pounds of green coffee in 2009. But what does 3 billion mean, exactly? For comparison, 3 billion seconds is 95 years. Jen St. Hilaire, the woman behind tiny Scarlet City Coffee Roasting, roasts less than 100 pounds of coffee a week. That's the difference between 100 seconds and 95 years.

Some of the most fun, exciting things in coffee are happening at the 100-second level. Geeky cellists, former data analysts, and tattooed urban homesteaders are roasting up tiny batches of coffee and selling them to friends, family, and intrepid coffee seekers online and at farmers' markets. Many of the roasters in this book, like Joel Domreis of Courier Coffee Roasters, began by roasting beans in their backyard and grew bit by bit until they were able to start their own companies. A few of the West Coast's littlest, least-known roasters:

Deep Cello, Badbeard's Microroastery
Portland, OR; deepcello.com, badbeardscoffee.com

Justin Kagan, a cellist with the Oregon Symphony, will serenade you with his medium-roasted blends and single origins, sold through two different brands. Available online.

Nectar Coffee Company
Portland, OR; nectarcoffeecompany.com

Todd Weiler has some serious coffee chops, having roasted for both Intelligentsia and Flying Goat. Now he roasts 5 pounds at a time and sells at Portland farmers' markets and online. (See also page 174.)

Scarlet City Coffee Roasting
Oakland, CA; scarletcityroasting.com

Jen St. Hilaire has been roasting coffee since 1995, churning out gorgeous espresso blends that she sells online and out of her small roastery in Oakland. (See also page 124.)

Velton's Coffee Roasting Company
Everett, WA; veltonscoffee.com

Like most microroasters, Velton's is a one-man show. But Velton Ross's exceptional coffees have a national following among the home barista community. His coffees are available online. (See also page 262.)

COURIER COFFEE ROASTERS

A COFFEE PHILOSOPHER AND HIS FRIENDS

The personable feel of Courier's downtown Portland café reflects how owner Joel Domreis got his start: roasting in his backyard with friends, then delivering mason jars of coffee to people's doorsteps by bike. (In fact, Domreis still takes orders by phone and will deliver by bike to inner-Portland residential and office addresses.) Friends remain at the core of his increasingly successful DIY business model: a friend made the café's hand-thrown ceramic mugs, a friend built the walnut bar, a friend helped him pour a new concrete floor. Domreis believes that quality has an ethical dimension and can be a way to measure happiness. Happy farmers pick the ripest coffee cherries, he contends, just like happy baristas take the greatest care in making coffee. As you might imagine, even black coffee is made by hand at Courier.

> COURIER COFFEE ROASTERS EMBODIES THE SCRAPPY, DIY ETHIC OF PORTLAND.

SIDLE UP TO THE BAR AND DRINK

Courier's coffee shop feels like a bar. The menu is a narrow sheath of brown paper, not unlike a cocktail menu. Everything is priced in full-dollar increments, and there's no cash register—bills are tabbed, and ones and fives are kept on a clipboard for making change. Domreis hates the fast-food–style line that forms at most cafés. He wants customers to be able to simply walk up to the bar and place an order. While your drink is made, you can watch or talk with the barista, often Domreis himself.

SINGLE ORIGINS, STRIKING FLAVORS

Courier carries two to eight coffees at a time depending on the harvest season. All are single origins, never blends. Domreis says he looks for coffees with clear, prominent flavors such as raspberry jam or sarsaparilla. He always seeks to balance the fruity, floral sweetness of the bean with the brown sugar or chocolaty flavors that come from caramelizing sugars during roasting. This balance of crispness and depth is the hallmark of what Domreis calls the Portland style, something he's proud to be associated with.

CAFÉ:
923 SW OAK ST.,
PORTLAND

ROASTING SINCE

'04

Less than 1000 lb./week

on a 25 lb. San Franciscan roaster

FIND THE COFFEE AT THEIR CAFÉ / YOUR DOORSTEP IN PORTLAND (BIKE DELIVERY)

EXTRACTO COFFEE ROASTERS

NOSTALGIC NEIGHBORHOOD CAFÉ

The Cadillac-blue La Marzocco four-group espresso machine that sits prominently on the bar at Extracto's original location may be the most beautiful machine in Portland. It combines well with dangling school-house lights and thick, wooden library chairs to give the café a slightly old-timey feel. Neighbors seem to flock here for a visit, catching up while they wait in out-the-door lines on weekend mornings. Extracto is a neighborhood coffee shop that just happens to roast excellent coffee. After serving other people's beans for three years, in 2008 owners Chris and Celeste Brady bought a 22-kilo Pro-bat drum roaster and began roasting their own. Now the indelible smell of fresh-roasting coffee is a regular part of the Extracto experience, beloved by loyal neighbors and coffee tourists from other parts of town.

THE SOUND OF BEAUTIFUL COFFEE

Chris Brady came to coffee via music. He worked as a barista to support a

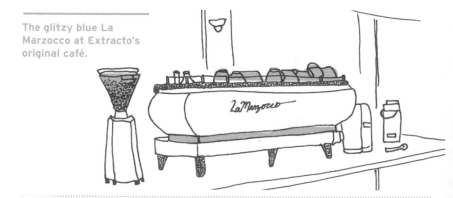

The glitzy blue La Marzocco at Extracto's original café.

music career with grunge-era band Pond. When he wasn't touring, he'd pick up shifts at the legendary Portland café Torrefazione Italia, an incubator of coffee fanaticism in the 1990s. Though he has traded in his bass for a Probat, Brady still understands the world—and coffee— through music. He likens building his signature espresso blend, Solutionary, to building a song. Brazilian and Indonesian coffees provide the bass line, Latin Americans the electric guitar, and Africans the cymbal clang. With components from Guatemala, Ethiopia, and Mexico, Solutionary is nutty with a hint of oranges (let's call it a Smiths song). No less great are carefully sourced single-origin coffees, especially the gentle, well-balanced Guatemala Finca Vista Hermosa (like a Nick Drake tune).

FROU-FROU-FREE COFFEE

In 2010 Extracto opened a smaller, quieter café about a mile from the first. There, the baristas prepare single cups of drip coffee at a custom-designed pour-over bar while you watch. But that's as frou-frou as Extracto gets. In a city sometimes known for getting caught up in what Brady calls the plumage of coffee culture, Extracto has only one yardstick for what it does: close your eyes, shut out the noise, and taste the coffee.

ROASTERY AND ORIGINAL CAFÉ:
2921 NE KILLINGSWORTH ST., PORTLAND

SECOND CAFÉ:
1465 NE PRESCOTT ST., PORTLAND

ROASTING SINCE '08

Less than 1000 lb./week — on a 22-kilo Probat roaster

FIND THE COFFEE AT EXTRACTOCOFFEE ROASTERS.COM / THEIR CAFÉS

AT EXTRACTO, GOOD COFFEE— LIKE A $10 BOTTLE OF WINE— IS FOR EVERYONE.

HEART COFFEE ROASTERS

INDUSTRIAL-ROMANTIC DECOR

It's hard not to crush on Heart's café, a cross between sleek European train station and rustic nineteenth-century science lab. Eclectic elements hang together in unexpected ways: Yellowing naturalist drawings of beetles hang opposite a hulking, industrial Probat roaster. A vintage rail station clock ticks calmly above the fray as baristas race behind a custom-painted, kelly green espresso machine. Black-and-white porcelain cups adorned with Finnish folk patterns perch above pristine white tile behind the bar. But the Continental aesthetic doesn't stop at design.

DELICATE ROASTS FROM THE NORDIC NATIONS

Owner and head roaster Wille Yli-Luoma (a Swedish-raised Finn) is fanatical for the Scandinavian approach

A SCANDINAVIAN APPROACH TO COFFEE, DELIVERED WITH QUINTESSENTIAL STYLE.

to coffee roasting. Didn't know Scandinavians had their own approach? Indeed. The top four countries in the world for highest coffee consumption per capita are Finland, Norway, Iceland, and Denmark. Folks in these northern, sun-starved nations love light-roasted coffee. The delicate approach is difficult to master, sometimes leading to the grassy or sour flavors of underroasting, but Yli-Luoma has worked hard to emulate masters like Denmark's Coffee Collective. Heart's single-origin coffees, like the juicy, blood-orangey Kenya Nyanja, are selected for lighter roasting. The signature Stereo espresso blend is a changing combination of in-season single-origin coffees (the package tells you which). Heart also prides itself on always offering single-origin espresso options in its café.

GADGETRY GALORE AND GENTLE GUIDANCE

Heart's clientele includes a disproportionately high number of service industry workers and off-shift baristas. They tolerate—and sometimes demand—a progressive approach to preparing coffee, so Heart has a deep roster of off-menu drip-bar offerings: Chemex, AeroPress, halogen siphon, and a unique German-designed coffee machine (an all-porcelain single cup brewer that produces a full-bodied cup). A barista might even offer to skim the crema off the top of your Americano (supposedly for sweetness) or suggest how long to wait before opening a bag of coffee at home (Yli-Luoma believes his coffees taste best two to three weeks after roasting). Heart's love affair with coffee is all-consuming, so who can blame them for dispensing relationship advice?

ROASTERY AND CAFÉ:
2211 EAST BURNSIDE ST., PORTLAND

ROASTING SINCE

'08

Less than 1000 lb./week

on a Probat UG15 roaster

FIND THE COFFEE AT HEARTROASTERS.COM / THEIR CAFÉ

KOBOS COFFEE

AN EARLY ALTERNATIVE TO MJB

Kobos Coffee has been around since the early days of the West Coast coffee boom. Way back in the 1970s, before anyone had heard of a latte, coffee people were just a casual, tight-knit community looking for something better than cheap, canned dreck. At the original Kobos store, customers scooped fresh-roasted beans out of burlap bags. At a time when most Americans thought coffee came in tins, tasted like watery dirt, and shouldn't cost more than $1 per pound, Kobos tried to convince them to spend a little more for better stuff. Photographs from the time show little wooden stakes sticking out of bagged coffee, reading, "Sumatra, $2.25/lb."

UPSCALE KITCHEN SUPPLIES

When David and Susan Kobos founded their company, it wasn't a

PORTLAND'S ORIGINAL CRAFT ROASTER IS ALIVE AND KICKING.

roastery but a high-end kitchen store supplying cookware, spices, coffee, and tea. It wasn't until David lucked into an old roasting machine that they found themselves in the coffee-roasting business. The modern roastery is still attached to a kitchen store and café, but it's a small vestige of the company's cookery heyday, when they had outposts across Portland.

BLENDS, VARIETALS, AND FLAVORED COFFEES

David Kobos's prized possession is a fire-engine-red, cast-iron Jabez Burns sample roaster from the 1930s. The computerless machine has no digital readouts—you measure the temperature by waving your hand in front of it—and reminds Kobos of the old days. He still roasts special blends for family and holiday gifts on the hip-height workhorse. Nowadays, most Kobos coffee is roasted to full city on semiautomatic 60-kilo machines. The company features blends, single origins, and some flavored coffees, which you'll find in grocery stores and restaurants around Portland. The company was one of the first Northwest roasters to be certified organic, and they continue to offer a deep menu of sustainable coffees. Co-owner Brian Dibble is the only man to sit on the board of directors of Cafe Femenino, an organization that supports women coffee farmers.

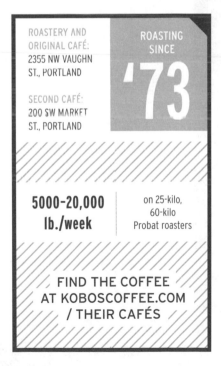

ROASTERY AND ORIGINAL CAFÉ:
2355 NW VAUGHN ST., PORTLAND

SECOND CAFÉ:
200 SW MARKET ST., PORTLAND

ROASTING SINCE

'73

5000–20,000 lb./week

on 25-kilo, 60-kilo Probat roasters

FIND THE COFFEE AT KOBOSCOFFEE.COM / THEIR CAFÉS

SUSTAINABLE COFFEE

One huge challenge coffee famers (and by implication coffee drinkers) will face in the coming decades is climate change, which is chasing coffee up the mountain and reducing yields for farmers worldwide. Sustainability is a very real concern for coffee roasters. Happily, there are many ways to be green when it comes to coffee.

ORGANIC COFFEE

A significant amount of coffee is organically grown, especially when it comes from the poorest coffee-growing countries, where pesticides are too expensive. But to be labeled organic, both roasters and growers must be certified, an expensive and time-consuming process. Organic certification is not a guarantee of quality, but some roasters, like Noble Coffee Roasting, do focus on high-quality organics. Many roasters make a point of carrying at least some organic coffees. Those that have long-term relationships with coffee farms can tell you quite a bit about how the coffee is grown and processed, regardless of whether it's certified.

ROASTING EQUIPMENT

Roasting coffee uses a lot of heat and therefore a lot of energy. That's why Equator Coffees & Teas switched to a Loring Smart Roaster, which uses 80 percent less energy than traditional drum roasters. Jeremy Adams of Cellar Door Coffee Roasters in Portland designed his own scrubbing system to clean the smoke produced during roasting using finely misted water (a big energy savings over traditional systems that burn the smoke).

BUILDINGS

Green buildings are expensive, so the roasters at the fore front of the green building trend are the biggies. In 2007 Peet's built the first LEED Gold-certified roasting plant in the country. Starbucks has made a commitment to build all new, company-owned cafés to LEED standards going forward. Batdorf & Bronson Coffee Roasters has taken a step in the right direction, adding solar panels to the roof of its roastery.

CARBON NEUTRALITY

Some sustainability-minded roasting companies go the extra mile to purchase offsets for their carbon use. Portland Roasting has purchased and planted nearly seventeen thousand trees to offset their carbon usage. Tiny Trailhead Coffee Roasters also purchases carbon offsets, though they are minimal given that all of their coffee is delivered by bike.

BIKE DELIVERY

Short of being 100 percent carbon neutral, many companies do what they can to reduce carbon emissions by delivering some or all of their coffee by bike. In Portland, Trailhead Coffee Roasters, Portland Roasting, Courier Coffee Roasters, and Clive Coffee deliver by bike. In San Francisco, De La Paz delivers much of its coffee by bike.

REUSABLE CUPS

Americans throw away twenty-three billion paper cups every year. Even using a compostable cup is no good if it gets thrown into a regular garbage can. If you can, always get your coffee in a for-here mug (it tastes better that way, too) or bring your own reusable cup.

BEYOND BEING GREEN

Sustainability of course extends far beyond recycling or even complex ecosystem management to include vastly complicated economic and social issues. Coffee roasting companies tackle these issues to varying degrees, but some have made it a core principal of their business. Portland Roasting and Thanksgiving Coffee Company have invested in projects tied to the UN's Millennium Development Goals, and Equator Coffees & Teas launched a food security project for orphans in Zimbabwe. The specialty coffee industry's relationship to sustainability becomes more intrinsic by the year, so expect these types of collaborations to become increasingly common.

Bike-friendly Trailhead Coffee
Roasters uses a custom-built
mobile coffee bar.

PORTLAND ROASTING COFFEE

ROOTED IN GLOBAL ACTIVISM

You're most likely to find Portland Roasting's coffee at local colleges and medium-sized socially conscious businesses like Burgerville, which for some reason makes the company seem much bigger than it actually is. Portland Roasting doesn't have a boutique retail café adorned with trendy reclaimed wood, but they do have a lot going on. Take a quick tour of their expansive website, and you'll learn as much about a project to rebuild an orphanage in the Aceh district of Sumatra as you will about the cinnamon, clove, and plum flavors of the organic coffee from that region. Owner Mark Stell fell in love with coffee as an activist and has remained true to those roots. After serving as a student delegate to the UN Earth Summit in Rio de Janeiro in 1992, he returned to Portland and started Abruzzi Coffee Roasters, an early microroasting operation in the city. It morphed into Portland Roasting in 1996.

AT PORTLAND ROASTING, COFFEE AND ADVOCACY GO HAND IN HAND.

INSIGHT COMES WITH OWNING A FARM

In 2007 Stell and his family went the extra mile to understand what it means to be in the coffee industry when his wife and brother purchased Ndovu Coffee Estate, a working 1500-acre coffee farm in Tanzania. They have poured money into improvements—investing in a new wet mill, planting young coffee trees, and building water storage for coffee processing. The experience has given Stell a lot of respect for what it takes to survive as a coffee grower. Working in Tanzania has also driven home the critical importance of water for local health and education, so Stell formed Portland Global Initiatives, a nonprofit that raises money for clean water access projects around East Africa.

Roasting you're certain to be getting a conscientious cup. Taste-wise, this is a coffee company for everyman, with comforting blends ranging from bright to brawny. Single-origin offerings, which tend to be roasted a touch lighter, include some top-quality beans from Kenya and Panama.

INDUSTRY-WIDE SUSTAINABILITY

All of that is relatively small potatoes compared to Stell's big goal: to measure the sustainability of the entire specialty-coffee industry, from carbon footprints to charitable giving and everything in between. Working closely with the Specialty Coffee Association of America, Stell orchestrated the launch of START (Sustainability Tracking and Reporting Tool), a massive data-tracking system used by roasters, cafés, importers, and organic and Fair Trade certification agencies to log piles of raw data on the industry. Sustainability projects and data management may seem far removed from the experience of drinking a mug of coffee, but with Portland

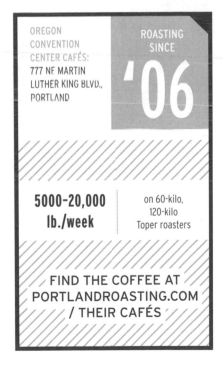

OREGON CONVENTION CENTER CAFÉS:
777 NE MARTIN LUTHER KING BLVD., PORTLAND

ROASTING SINCE '06

5000–20,000 lb./week

on 60-kilo, 120-kilo Toper roasters

FIND THE COFFEE AT PORTLANDROASTING.COM / THEIR CAFÉS

RISTRETTO ROASTERS

RISTRETTO DELIVERS A RARE, WELL-ROUNDED COFFEE EXPERIENCE.

KEY PLAYER IN THE LOCAL SCENE

In Portland, Ristretto Roasters was once David to Stumptown's Goliath. From 1999 to 2004, Stumptown dominated the city's coffee landscape with their hipster-inflected, visionary approach. Enter Din Johnson, a former contractor with a home-roasting hobby. When Ristretto opened the doors to its minuscule roastery and café in the Beaumont neighborhood in 2005, it paved the way for the full flowering of Portland's roasting scene, which has coffee lovers around the country sitting up and paying atten-

tion. In Ristretto's wake came Extracto, Cellar Door, Courier, Coava, Sterling, and many more.

FRIENDLY CAFÉS, HAPPY WORKERS

The original café remains a neighborhood favorite, but in 2009, with the help of a respected local architecture firm, Ristretto opened a second location in North Portland with some serious sex appeal. Its airy open bar floats under soaring ceilings. At both cafés (as well as a third in Northwest Portland, opened in 2012) the atmosphere is warm and welcoming, not snobby in the least. The baristas, besides being skilled, are clearly happy. And why shouldn't they be? Ristretto offers health insurance to its employees (exceptional for a coffee company of its size). It further distinguishes itself with the quality of its edible goodies—raspberry compote and ginger muffins, anyone?—made by nationally recognized pastry chef Kim Boyce, formerly of Spago in Los Angeles. Johnson's wife, Nancy Rommelmann, is a freelance journalist and runs a well-regarded reading series out of the Williams café, featuring respected local and visiting authors.

SINGLE ORIGINS AND POWERFUL ESPRESSOS

The house espresso blend, Beaumont, has a chocolaty base with jammy fruit flavors layered on top. As the company name implies, if you order straight espresso, expect to receive it ristretto (short), with intensely condensed flavors. Single origins from Guatemala, Nicaragua, Uganda, and elsewhere rotate through the menu and can be ordered as espresso. Having focused for years on coffee roasting and preparation, Johnson is now traveling more. By visiting coffee-growing regions and building relationships with growers, he hopes to connect his work at the end of the coffee chain with growers' work at the beginning of it.

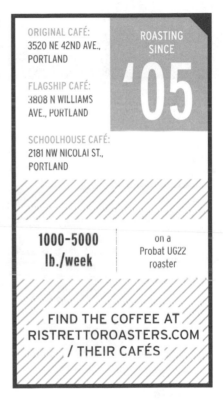

ORIGINAL CAFÉ:
3520 NE 42ND AVE.,
PORTLAND

FLAGSHIP CAFÉ:
3808 N WILLIAMS
AVE., PORTLAND

SCHOOLHOUSE CAFÉ:
2181 NW NICOLAI ST.,
PORTLAND

ROASTING SINCE
'05

1000-5000 lb./week

on a Probat UG22 roaster

FIND THE COFFEE AT RISTRETTOROASTERS.COM / THEIR CAFÉS

SPELLA CAFFÈ

CAFÉ: 520 SW 5TH AVE., PORTLAND	ROASTING SINCE '08
Less than 1000 lb./week	on a 5-kilo US Roaster Corp roaster
FIND THE COFFEE AT THEIR CAFÉ	

A SIMPLE EXTRAVAGANCE

Despite its simplicity, Spella Caffè might provide the most elegant coffee experience in Portland. Drawing on a background in food and a deep appreciation for high-quality service, Andrea Spella created a tiny, standing-room-only café in downtown Portland where you are treated like royalty. It might take ten minutes or more to order a double espresso, watch it being made, and drink it—but those minutes feel like a little vacation. From the warm, friendly service (including the no-attitude-allowed provision of sugar for your macchiato), to the day's paper resting on the bar, to the on-tap chaser of fizzy water, Spella has worked out the tiny details that elevate coffee to a true luxury.

SPELLA CAFFÈ PRESENTS A TAKE ON ITALIAN TRADITIONS WITH RESTRAINT AND STYLE.

ROASTING TO SECOND CRACK

Andrea Spella was too young to take over his family's bakery business before it was sold, so instead of becoming a baker, he educated his palate as a restaurant manager and sommelier. He prefers espresso blends composed of three or four unique, high-quality coffees instead of the traditional Italian recipes that use up to a dozen. But he does follow the old-style Italian approach to roasting slower at lower temperatures, which discourages the intensity of certain acids from developing. Spella roasts most coffees to the door of second crack, or full city plus, which is relatively uncommon among Portland's microroasters. It gives his espresso blend a sweet, mellow crème brûlée flavor. Every other coffee on offer is a single origin. Spella especially favors beans from the Antigua region of Guatemala, which tend to be mild

and consistent, offering a classic coffee flavor that is neither too earthy, too bright, nor too fruity.

HAND-PULLED ESPRESSO

Spella Caffè has one of the only hand-pulled lever espresso machines in the Northwest. The theatrical method hasn't changed much since the modern espresso was invented in 1947 in Italy. Instead of merely pressing a button, the barista uses his entire body to carefully pull a lever on the machine down, which draws hot water into a piston chamber. When it's released, pressurized water is forced through the coffee grounds, and out comes a perfect ristretto shot. The method involves physicality, intuition, and focus. Watching the barista throw his entire body into working the lever (it's quite difficult), you know you're getting something made with love and attention.

STERLING COFFEE ROASTERS

FROM TINY TO TONY

In 2009 barista Adam McGovern and a partner opened Portland's smallest microroastery. Under the name Sterling, they roasted one pound of coffee at a time on a copper-colored San Franciscan, serving it up at an elegant open-air counter. Sterling has a bigger roasting machine now, and the open air counter is in limbo (check the website for current information). Thankfully, McGovern is also the owner of Coffeehouse NW, a gorgeous light-filled corner café with exposed brick walls and floor-to-ceiling windows. The café employs some of Portland's best and most nattily dressed baristas (think gents in ties and waistcoats; ladies in satiny blouses). Coffeehouse NW now exclusively serves Sterling's coffees, with customary precision and style.

"TELL YA WHAT, THERE'S NUTHIN' BETTER ON A SUNDAY MORNIN' THAN A LITTLE YVES SAINT CROISSANT WITH A FRANK SUMATRA ACCOMPANIMENT."

AN EDUCATION, WITH HUMOR

Sterling's curated offerings include just two single-origin coffees at a time, one from Latin America and one from Africa. (If you order a latte, you'll get the Latin American coffee by default, with more typically chocolaty or nutty flavors that go well with milk. For a straight shot of espresso, you have your pick.) Over a year, Sterling features twenty-five different coffees, with the menu changing every month. Regulars are treated to an informal education as they spend a fortnight with one coffee and move on to another, learning along the way to distinguish between, for example, the flavors of a Bolivian versus a Colombian high-grown varietal. McGovern keeps things from getting too serious by including whimsical flavor descriptions ("Heath Bar starfruit," "berry mélange") and by posting clever daily photos and epigrams on Sterling's Facebook page.

A SCIENTIFIC APPROACH TO ROASTING

The beautiful copper San Franciscan sample roaster is still in service, churning out sample roasts one pound at a time. McGovern takes a scientific approach, rigorously testing every new coffee with four different profiles to find the best match before bringing it into full production.

COFFEEHOUSE NORTHWEST:
1951 W BURNSIDE ST.,
PORTLAND

ROASTING SINCE
'09

Less than 1000 lb./week

on 1 lb. San Franciscan and 5-kilo US Roaster Corp. roasters

FIND THE COFFEE AT COFFEEHOUSE NORTHWEST

STUMPTOWN COFFEE ROASTERS

ROASTERY AND ORIGINAL CAFÉ:
4525 SE DIVISION ST., PORTLAND

ROASTING SINCE '99

ANNEX:
3352 SE BELMONT ST., PORTLAND

5000-20,000 lb./week

on a 60-kilo Probat roaster (Portland)

on a 45-kilo Probat roaster (New York)

on a 22-kilo Probat roaster (Seattle)

FIND THE COFFEE AT STUMPTOWNCOFFEE.COM / THEIR CAFÉS COAST TO COAST

QUICK RISE TO THE TOP

When Stumptown founder Duane Sorenson enters a room, he leads with ample gut. The kingpin of indie coffee has occasion to strut: beginning in 1999 with a small café and a tiny 5-kilo roaster, he built Stumptown into an internationally respected boutique coffee company. Stumptown's coffee buyers slurp on average 166 spoonfuls of up to twenty different coffees each day. They spend nine months each year in twenty different coffee-producing countries, visiting some farms as many as three times annually. In 2011 Stumptown brought in a major investor to help fund the opening of roasteries

FROM A QUIET RESIDENTIAL STREET IN PORTLAND, STUMPTOWN LAUNCHED A TATTOO-SPORTING, BEER-GUZZLING, HEAVY-METAL-LOVING, GEEKED-OUT COFFEE REVOLUTION.

and cafés in new cities and expand the reach of its bottled, cold-brewed coffee. The move caused devotees to question whether Stumptown still qualified as an indie coffee company, and sent others scrambling to decode what it might mean for the future of high-end specialty coffee. Love it or hate it, it's just one more example of how Stumptown can't seem to shake the spotlight.

A PIONEER IN TRANSPARENCY

Stumptown's website includes extensive information about the farms and co-ops they buy coffee from. This focus is only fitting, since they helped pioneer transparent supply chains. The status quo in the coffee trade once involved exporters and importers jealously guarding information about where their highest-quality coffees came from, or those same coffees being unceremoniously dumped together with lower-quality beans. Now, thanks to the work of Sorenson and others, lot separation is standard and information is not only public but has become a defining element of third-wave coffee, with many roasters listing farms, producers, elevation, and varietal on every bag of beans. Indeed, some farms have themselves achieved brand status, like Panama Esmeralda. The best lots of the Geisha varietal grown there, labeled Esmeralda Especial, have garnered some of the highest prices ever paid for coffee at auction—and Stumptown has won bids more than once. (The coffee has retailed for as much as $200 per pound.) Nearly a third of Stumptown's offerings come out of

At the Annex, Stumptown showcases all their current coffees,
which you can buy by the cup or
take home.

extensive, multiyear relationships with coffee producers. When the company begins a project with a farm, they generally make significant demands to get and maintain the highest quality, sometimes asking farmers to drastically alter how they harvest and process their coffees. Farmers acquiesce because Stumptown pays a premium to help them shoulder the risk.

ONE HAIRBENDER, MANY SINGLE ORIGINS

The Hairbender espresso blend, known for its no-holds-barred mix of citrus and chocolate flavors, is Stumptown's biggest seller by far. The ubiquity of Hairbender in Portland since 1999 has shaped the taste preferences of an entire generation of coffee lovers in the city, with ripple effects up and down the West Coast. But despite the prominence of one blend, Stumptown is really a single-origin coffee company, offering twenty to thirty different coffees from around the world. They are known for discovering outstanding and unusual coffees in little-known places, like Burundi, and spending years to bring them to consumers. They were also pivotal in

popularizing lighter roasting and its way of showcasing the unique terroir of single origins. This approach, which now dominates the indie coffee world, has spread partly as Stumptown has moved into new cities.

STRAIGHT COFFEE, NO CREAM

Part of Stumptown's success has to do with its aura of intractable cool—hipster baristas, art shows, turntables, and the like. But in the end it's the coffee that counts, and the most undiluted experience of Stumptown's coffee can be had at Portland's Annex location. There you'll find the current lineup in its entirety. You can order a single cup of any coffee, but milk and cream are absent, as are espresso machines. It's more like a temple than a café, with large glass jars of coffee lining one wall and every imaginable trend-forward home coffee-making device on the opposite wall, marvels of stainless steel, ceramic, and glass. It's the best place on the West Coast to see the full range of Stumptown's accomplishment. (On the other coast, a similar setup prevails at the Red Hook roastery in Brooklyn.)

TRAILHEAD COFFEE ROASTERS

INSPIRED BY THE GREAT OUTDOORS

Ordering a cup of coffee at Trailhead is a unique experience. You're almost certainly outside, perhaps standing in a light Portland rain. A little Bialetti moka pot sits atop the open flame of a camp stove. And in lieu of a counter, your barista stands behind a 110-pound, custom-built Metrofiets bike. That's Charlie Wicker preparing one of his small-batch-roasted coffees. Trailhead is named for Wicker's vision of the perfect coffee experience: a cup enjoyed outdoors on a freezing morning after a long night's sleep on the cold, hard ground. He brings the vision alive by setting up his coffee bike on Portland's bridges for early-morning bike commuters, or at the finish lines of local cycling races. He even rode it on a 500-mile trip across eastern Oregon, serving coffee to fellow riders along the way.

BIKE DELIVERIES AND CARBON OFFSETS

Wicker doesn't have a café and mostly gives away the coffee he prepares on the bike—a savvy marketing ploy. He sells most of his coffee to local cafés and grocery stores (all listed on his website). During his days as a data analyst, Wicker couldn't bear sitting still for long periods, so naturally he delivers to most of his clients by bike. In addition, he purchases carbon offsets to make the business entirely carbon neutral.

EVERYTHING—BUT ESPECIALLY COFFEE—TASTES BETTER AFTER A DAY ON THE TRAIL.

SUPPORTING WOMEN AND COMMUNITIES

Wicker calls the coffee bean a simple vehicle for change, and the coffee business an "elegant commerce." He believes coffee should be produced and sold in ways that benefit people, but not as a matter of charity. As part of his commitment to strengthening communities, he buys much of his coffee from Cafe Femenino. The coffee is grown by women around the world, and premiums are put back into social programs benefiting women farmers. Wicker also invests a share of his profits in Kiva microloans to individual women. Regular coffees include the Summit and Switchback roasts (from Mexico and Bolivia, respectively) and the Gravity espresso blend. Trailhead's coffees tend to have the chocolaty, nutty, and candylike flavors typical of full city roasts.

ROASTING SINCE

'08

Less than 1000 lb./week

on a Diedrich IR-12 roaster

FIND THE COFFEE AT THEIR MOBILE CAFÉ / FULL LIST OF LOCATIONS AT TRAILHEAD COFFEEROASTERS.COM

WATER AVENUE COFFEE COMPANY

ELEGANCE AMID INDUSTRY

While enjoying a silky cappuccino at Water Avenue Coffee Company, you might feel the walls and floor shudder slightly. Yes, the coffee's that good—but what you're feeling is a freight train passing a mere block away. Water Avenue is one of a growing number of upscale bars and restaurants situated among a tangle of highway overpasses and jangling rail lines in a still-thriving industrial area. The railway and Water Avenue serve the industrial zone's produce wholesalers, freight companies, and distilleries. From glistening, hundred-year-old wood counters reclaimed from a local warehouse, to an enormous blue neon sign reading simply "coffee" (visible from the highway overpass above), it's clear the folks at Water Avenue aim to honor the neighborhood's history, even as they eagerly look to the future.

> WATER AVENUE HONORS THE WORKING-CLASS ROOTS OF PORTLAND'S INNER SOUTHEAST INDUSTRIAL ZONE.

GEEKY BUT DOWN-TO-EARTH

Water Avenue may be a destination shop, attracting coffee lovers from across the city and region, but it doesn't like to sneer. Connected to the American Barista and Coffee School, the roastery-café excels at gentle education in a warm, casual atmosphere. And despite having one of the geekiest pour-over programs on the West Coast, they know neighborhood regulars often need a quick fix, so they keep an airpot with freshly brewed black coffee at the ready. If you like your coffee with a bit of education on the side, the baristas—who get regular training on all aspects of the business—can break down their approach, so you can try to make your own perfect cup at home.

UNIQUE ROASTER, UNIQUE FLAVORS

Water Avenue's coffee is roasted on a Samiac, a rare drum roaster from France. The roaster, built in 1974, gives an unusual flavor profile to a medley of single-origin beans, most of them microlots from well-regarded farms around the world. It is especially good at producing the kind of clean, bright flavors that are harder to achieve with drum roasters (this is because the Samiac can be adjusted to allow more air to flow around the roasting beans). The signature El Toro espresso blend is mild, with chocolate flavor, floral aroma, and a hint of spice in the finish.

ROASTERY AND CAFÉ:
1028 SE WATER AVE.
#145, PORTLAND

ROASTING SINCE
'09

1000–5000
lb./week

on 20-kilo Samiac and Probatino roasters

FIND THE COFFEE AT
WATERAVENUECOFFEE.COM
/ THEIR CAFÉ

10-SPEED COFFEE ROASTERS

SERVING UP COFFEE IN THREE OF THE COLUMBIA GORGE'S MOST BEAUTIFUL OUTDOORSY SPOTS, 10-SPEED KEEPS YOU MOVING.

FRESH-ROASTED COFFEE THE LOCALS LOVE

Hood River, tucked into a valley on the Columbia Gorge just 60 miles east of Portland, is a year-round destination for city dwellers to the west. They come for the outdoor recreation—windsurfing, skiing, cycling—and the orchards (Hood River County grows more Anjou pears than any other county in the U.S., tens of millions each year). For a town of only seven thousand, Hood River boasts a thriving coffee culture, with stellar cafés among its wineries, restaurants, and fancy shops. But head just west of downtown's tourist action and you'll find 10-Speed, whose small-batch-roasted coffees have earned it a devoted following.

FUNKY STOP FOR BIKE ENTHUSIASTS

As you might guess from the company name, Hood River has its fair share of hardcore bicyclists. One of them is 10-Speed owner Bryan McGeeney, who owns more bicycles than there are days in the week. McGeeney and a partner opened a second café five miles up the road in Mosier, a tiny farming community that just happens to sit right on one of the best cycling roads in the country (the nocars-allowed Historic Columbia River Highway). The café is a funky old shack serving beer, wine, and food in addition to lattes. Laid-back baristas serve up double shots for casual weekend riders, or for the hundreds that come through on miniature Tour de France–style stage races in the summer. In 2011 McGeeney forded across the Columbia to open a third location in another rural community, White Salmon, Washington, which serves as a jumping-off point for whitewater adventures on the White Salmon River.

SINGLE ORIGINS AND LOW-KEY GEEKERY

10-Speed has only one blend, Kickstand, a mellow mix of Brazilian, Sumatran, and Ethiopian beans. Otherwise the focus is on single-origin microlots. The menu board shows six to seven coffees at a time, each identified by origin and flavor profile. A coffee from the Rwandan Abakundakawa cooperative, for example, is described as having "initial notes of orange zest and sweet tea, and a finish of hibiscus and honey." Every cup is prepared by hand in a classic example of low-key geekery: the pour-over bar is built using toilet flanges from the hardware store.

ROASTERY AND FLAGSHIP CAFÉ: 1235 STATE ST., HOOD RIVER

ROASTING SINCE '05

Less than 1000 lb./week

on a 5-kilo Probat roaster

FIND THE COFFEE AT THEIR HOOD RIVER, MOSIER, AND WHITE SALMON CAFÉS

BACKPORCH COFFEE ROASTERS

ROASTERY AND SHOWCASE CAFÉ: 70 SW CENTURY DR., SUITE 130, BEND	ROASTING SINCE '04
ORIGINAL CAFÉ: 1052 NW NEWPORT AVE., BEND	

Less than 1000 lb./week	on a Diedrich IR-12 roaster

FIND THE COFFEE AT BACKPORCHCOFFEE ROASTERS.COM / THEIR CAFÉS

BIG-CITY COFFEE MINUS THE EGO

At a turn in the Deschutes River, where ponderosa pines give way to the Oregon high desert plateau, sits central Oregon's modest-sized metropolis: Bend. Located on the cloudless side of the Cascades, Bend offers ample sun and proximity to snow, attracting outdoor lovers from around the Northwest. Backporch Coffee Roasters is one of a growing number of small roasters in the town, which tripled in population between 1990 and 2010. Backporch has two cafés on the west side of the city, just out of earshot of downtown's hustle-bustle. Though the coffee is as good as what you'd find in a bigger city, one vestige of urban coffee culture is deliciously absent: the attitude. Backporch even makes its own flavored syrups. And if you're going to cover up your coffee with milk and syrup, it might as well be a homemade salted caramel syrup.

MODERN, WITH A NOD TO HISTORY

In 2011 Backporch opened a showcase café at the site of the former Brightwood lumber mill. Some of the café's details evoke the site's origins, such as the custom wood tables and shelving reclaimed from a nearby hundred-year-old barn. Other touches, like the crisp white walls and tin paneled bar, offer a chill modern contrast. A flirty trail of stenciled airplanes winds along the length of the wall opposite the bar, honoring a toy plane manufacturing plant that once inhabited the site. Follow the trail toward the back of the shop and you'll find Backporch's pot of proverbial gold: a perky red Diedrich drum roaster.

TWO-WAY ROAD BETWEEN FARM AND CAFÉ

Backporch offers a sophisticated menu of medium-roasted single-origin coffees and one signature blend. Owners Dave and Majell Beach have traveled to coffee farms to learn how coffee is grown and processed. Backporch is proud to feature a small number of direct trade coffees, including a juicy offering from El Salvador's Las Delicias plantation. The farm is owned by brothers Miguel and Guillermo Menéndez, who have made the rare reverse trek to the Northwest to see how their coffee is prepared and enjoyed at Backporch.

BACKPORCH KEEPS BEND'S GROWING POPULATION BUZZING.

LONE PINE COFFEE ROASTERS

URBANE COFFEE
IN THE
HIGH DESERT.

A LITTLE SURPRISE TO SAVOR

When you pass an alley in Bend's charming historic downtown, look for a little sign that reads, simply, "coffee." Tucked away on Tin Pan Alley, a small crosscut, you'll find the central city's only coffee roaster: Lone Pine. From the little alleyway entrance, to little tables snuggled together, and the squat little roaster in the back, Lone Pine feels like a secret you can hold under your tongue. The European sensibility of the café comes in part from the way everything is scaled down, modest, and lived-in. The new café even holds a piece of Northwest coffee history: the hand-painted, ceramic-top tables come from Portland's famed Torrefazione Italia café, where Scott Witham earned his chops as a barista before he and his wife, Anna Witham, ever dreamed of becoming coffee roasters.

SEASONAL BLEND, SINGLE ORIGINS

A wall behind the bar is covered in rapturous euphemisms for coffee: "The intellectual drink. A restorative of sparkling wit. King of all perfumes." That may give you a sense of how the owners feel about the stuff. Scott Witham roasts the coffee onsite with a red Diedrich IR-12. He is constantly tweaking the Heartwood espresso blend, which at any time contains two in-season coffees—one iteration included Brazilian and Guatemalan coffees from the Pedro Rossi and Las Magnolias farms, respectively. Regardless of the season or ingredients, the blend aims for a balance between cocoa, hazelnut, and toffee flavors. The modest menu also includes one dark-roasted coffee and a small clutch of single origins.

EXTRA-CREAMY, FARM-FRESH MILK

When Mark Twain wrote that he longed for "American coffee, with real cream," he didn't mean the stuff you buy at the grocery store. He meant the cream-on-top stuff fresh from the cow, with its rich, sweet flavor and silky mouthfeel. Unlike the vast majority of American cafés, Lone Pine purchases farm-fresh, organic, nonhomogenized, glass-bottled milk for its lattes, cappuccinos, and mochas. To get the right texture when the milk is steamed, baristas first shake the bottles vigorously. The milk travels from Noris Dairy in the Willamette Valley, up and over the Cascade Range.

ROASTERY AND ORIGINAL CAFÉ:
845 TIN PAN ALLEY, BEND

ROASTING SINCE

'07

Less than 1000 lb./week

on a Diedrich IR-12 roaster

FIND THE COFFEE AT LONEPINECOFFEE.COM / THEIR CAFÉ

ASHLAND

NOBLE COFFEE ROASTING

ELEGANT ROAST IN A SMALL TOWN

Ashland is an Oregon hamlet known for its productions of *Hamlet*—it's the home of the prestigious Oregon Shakespeare Festival. Along with a thriving restaurant scene, Ashland has a handful of good coffee shops, but none perform like Noble Coffee Roasting. The roastery-café, located just off the beaten path in the railroad district, attracts locals and theater tourists in equal measure. Noble goes big in this cultured small town, with exposed ceiling joists, chalkboard menus, made-by-the-cup siphon brewing, and naked portafilters. But that's all gloss on the real attraction: some of the only carefully sourced and beautifully roasted coffee available between Portland and San Francisco. Theatergoers can also grab a preshow latte at Noble's walk-up window, near downtown's theater complex.

IN THE THEATER CAPITAL OF OREGON, NOBLE PUTS COFFEE CENTER STAGE.

WELL-TAILORED ESPRESSO (AND BEER)

Drinks at Noble are not "as you like it." No hot milkshakes here—nothing bigger than 16 ounces, no syrups beyond vanilla and almond. It's much ado about all the right things. Noble tailors its blends specifically for espresso and lattes. The Pompadour, a more lightly roasted mix of

African and Latin American coffees, is used for straight espresso. The World Tour is a spicy, chocolaty espresso blend perfect in a latte. A classic Mokha Java combines Ethiopian and Sumatran coffees for a bright, earthy cup. Also on tap? How about a pint of Noble Stout, a beer from Standing Stone Brewing Company made using cold-brewed Mokha Java.

TOP-NOTCH COFFEES, ALL ORGANIC

Owner Jared Rennie is a former high school Spanish teacher who uses his language skills when working directly with growers, judging Cup of Excellence competitions, and visiting countries of origin to learn more about farming and processing methods. He sources only organic and sustainably grown coffees, a relatively unique focus in the world of high-end coffee. His goal is to demonstrate that organic and quality are not mutually exclusive. Noble's menu of outstanding seasonal single origins— such as the award-winning Kiaora, the first certified organic Kenyan coffee available in the U.S.—are proof that he's succeeding.

ROASTERY AND ORIGINAL CAFÉ:
281 FOURTH ST., ASHLAND

WALK-UP WINDOW:
46 E MAIN ST., ASHLAND

ROASTING SINCE
'07

1000-5000 lb./week

on a Probat L12 roaster

FIND THE COFFEE AT NOBLECOFFEEROASTING.COM / THEIR CAFÉS

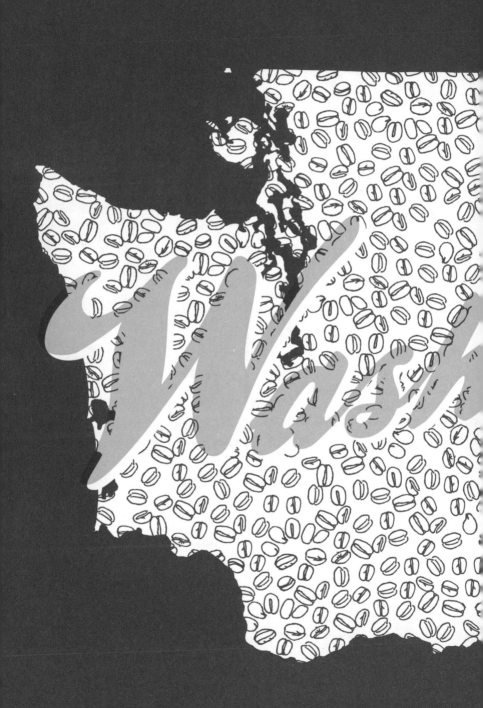

Since the 1980s, coffee has been synonymous with Seattle in the public imagination (though it has lost some pride of place as other cities have stepped up their game). Coffee wormed its way into the fabric of city life during Seattle's grunge-era heyday, and the city's coffee culture has remained much the same as it was then. Roasting is no exception. Seattle remains unabashedly an espresso town, with a preference for darker roasts and blends. Old hands and newcomers alike, from Espresso Vivace to Herkimer, diligently, tirelessly churn out beautiful shots built from carefully crafted blends.

The city is home to a huge number of passionate, old-school experts. Washington in general remains the epicenter of coffee technology on the West Coast, home to leading companies like Synesso, La Marzocco, and Espresso

Parts Northwest. Meanwhile, a few newer roasters are pushing Seattleites to reconsider drip coffee and espresso through the lens of more lightly roasted single origins.

The rest of Washington, with a few notable exceptions along the I-5 corridor, suffers a similar fate as exurbs and rural areas everywhere. Washington State is the spiritual home of the drive-through espresso stand and its seedier second-cousin, the bikini barista stand (in which a severely underclad young woman in a dainty Santa outfit or pasties prepares your triple caramel nonfat mocha). Further proof that Washingtonians love coffee with a seemingly inexhaustible, um, passion.

SEATTLE

SEATTLE

SEATTLE

TLE SEAT

TTLE SEAT

SEATTLE

CAFFÉ D'ARTE

CAFFÉ D'ARTE HAS REMAINED HUMBLY UNTRENDY SINCE 1985, STICKING WITH A TRADITIONAL APPROACH THAT DRAWS ON ITS FOUNDER'S ROOTS IN ITALY.

THE DEFINITION OF ESPRESSO

In the late 1970s, when only a handful of Starbucks cafés could be found in Seattle, Mauro Cipolla's family would drive to Vancouver, British Columbia, to buy espresso once a month. The recent immigrants from Milan couldn't stand Seattle's drip coffee, which they called "dirty water." Cipolla returned to Italy to apprentice with a master roaster and in 1985 formed Caffé D'arte to bring southern Italian–style espresso to America. The medium-sized roastery helped define what Northwesterners thought espresso should look and taste like—dark, thick-bodied, and sweet with an edge of bitterness.

TRUE TO THE OLD WAYS

D'arte's roastmasters follow tradition-al recipes for Italian espresso. Starting with a heavy base of Brazilian beans, they add Mexican and Indonesian coffees for body. Over the years the roasts have gotten subtly darker as popular tastes have changed, but little else has been impacted by the whims of consumers. They didn't capitulate to calls for flavored coffee in the 1990s, they don't sell single-origin coffees or market their decades-long relationships with coffee farms, and their packaging remains much the same as it was in the 1980s. D'arte is also proud to operate a wood-fired drum roasting machine, a 1949 Balestra, just like the one Cipolla learned to roast on. Spicy smoke from hand-chopped alder wood is drawn across the beans as they roast, giving the coffee a predictably woodsy flavor.

SOCCER FANS ONE AND ALL

Perhaps unsurprisingly in a company where half the employees are Italian or Latino, Caffé D'arte is fanatical about fútbol. Two of the owners, Jeff Stock and Mark Schuur, played for the Seattle Sounders and University of Washington, respectively, in the 1970s and 1980s. Head roaster and green buyer Joe Mancuso played for

University of Nevada, Las Vegas, and was a member of the national under-20 team. When the World Cup rolls around, flatscreen TVs are installed in the production facility so that employees can watch the games—a ploy that's as much about camaraderie as about making sure everyone shows up for work. Caffé D'arte also supports local youth sports through annual fundraisers.

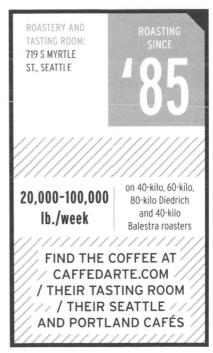

ROASTERY AND TASTING ROOM:
719 S MYRTLE ST., SEATTLE

ROASTING SINCE '85

20,000–100,000 lb./week

on 40-kilo, 60-kilo, 80-kilo Diedrich and 40-kilo Balestra roasters

FIND THE COFFEE AT CAFFEDARTE.COM / THEIR TASTING ROOM / THEIR SEATTLE AND PORTLAND CAFÉS

CAFFÈ UMBRIA

A REFLECTION OF MODERN ITALY

In contrast to romanticized, nostalgic visions of Italy, Caffè Umbria has built two sleek, modern cafés that reflect the style and culture of the country as it actually exists. Both locations, in Seattle and Portland, include black granite counters and sweeping curves of wood and stainless steel. Stand-up bars let you toss back a quick espresso between business meetings, like Italians do. Exposed bricks and lovely lighting add a touch of warmth, as do charming black-and-white photographs from the Bizzarri family.

THIRD-GENERATION ROASTMASTER

Owner and roaster Emanuele Bizzarri comes from a family of coffee masters. His grandfather Ornello roasted coffee in Umbria, Italy, after World

OLD-WORLD FLAVORS AND HIGH EUROPEAN STYLE COME TOGETHER AT CAFFÈ UMBRIA.

War II. His father, Umberto, founded legendary Torrefazione Italia in Seattle in 1986—in fact, the Seattle Umbria café is located in the original Torrefazione. Umbria, like Torrefazione before it, is deeply entrenched in the Italian approach to coffee, which extends far beyond a focus on traditional blends and espresso that "caresses." Careful café design, professional baristas, and touches like live broadcasts of Italian soccer matches evoke the rich role that coffee plays in Italian culture. And since nothing is as Italian as food, Caffè Umbria serves Italian-style panini, gelato, and traditional specialty drinks. The *cioccolato caldo*, nearly as thick as pudding, will warm your soul on a blustery day.

OLD-WORLD ESPRESSO BLENDS

Hewing to the Italian tradition, Umbria's focus is firmly on espresso. The company offers five blends and no single-origin coffees. If you order an espresso drink you'll get the Gusto Crema, the most popular coffee they offer. It is supremely mild in flavor, as inoffensive as a shot of espresso gets. For drip, they offer four additional blends, including the more darkly roasted Arco Etrusco. Though Umbria's coffee is showcased in its two glossy cafés, most of their coffee is actually sold to restaurants, offices, hotels, and other cafés across the Northwest and U.S.

SHOWCASE CAFÉ.
320 OCCIDENTAL
AVE. S, SEATTLE

PORTLAND CAFÉ:
303 NW 12TH AVE.,
PORTLAND

ROASTING
SINCE
'02

5000-20,000
lb./week

on an
STA Impianti RE 60
roaster

FIND THE COFFEE AT
CAFFEUMBRIA.COM
/ THEIR SEATTLE AND
PORTLAND CAFÉS

CAFFÉ VITA
COFFEE ROASTING COMPANY

ROASTERY AND CAFÉ:
1005 E PIKE ST., SEATTLE

ROASTING SINCE
'95

20,000-100,000 lb./week

on 45-kilo, 60-kilo Probat roasters

FIND THE COFFEE AT CAFFEVITA.COM / THEIR SEATTLE, OLYMPIA, AND PORTLAND CAFÉS

BORN IN MID-1990S SEATTLE

Way back in the Stone Age of specialty coffee—1995—three Mikes (McConnell, Prins, and Foster) banded together to form a different kind of Seattle coffee-roasting company: smaller in scale and focused on quality. Their name, logo (Punichello, the trickster character), and roasting style all drew on traditional Italian coffee culture, a reflection of the founders' travels. But Caffé Vita's growing success was firmly rooted in the culture and aesthetic of mid-1990s Seattle. The look was dark, masculine, a little on edge; the coffee was mostly espresso; and the cafés were located in the city's most vibrant cultural outposts, beginning in Queen Anne.

LOCAL DEVOTION, EXPLOSIVE GROWTH

Vita didn't just reflect the culture of Seattle when it first opened—it helped create it. Besides roasting and serving their own coffee, the company sponsored numerous underground arts and music events, even forming its own record label. It also partnered with numerous nonprofits, earning it lots of local love. In contrast to its humble beginnings, Vita has become a major coffee-roasting company in Seattle; its coffee is served in hundreds of local cafés and restaurants across the Northwest. Caffé Vita now operates eight cafés: six in Seattle, one in Portland, and one in Olympia. Their Public Brewing School, operating out of the Pike Street location in Seattle, offers free monthly classes on making coffee at home.

RUSTICALLY SWEET, SILKY

Despite enormous growth, Vita's brand and coffee haven't changed much. As with most Seattle roasters, the focus has never wavered from espresso. Their espresso blends have backbone and a rustic sweetness,

NOW ONE OF SEATTLE'S BIGGEST ROASTERS, CAFFÉ VITA STARTED SMALL—JUST THREE GUYS NAMED MIKE.

shying away from unusual flavors or too much citrus. Caffe Del Sol, the house espresso blend of Latin American, African, and Indonesian coffees, is silky, with cocoa and praline flavors. Most intriguing is a blend developed in partnership with Seattle-based Theo Chocolates. The coffee was designed to evoke the taste of chocolate, with flavors of vanilla and tobacco, and mate well with Theo's coffee-flavored confections, including a salted coffee caramel and a coffee and dark chocolate bar. There's no better place to overload your endorphins than at the bustling Caffé Vita in Capitol Hill, where a huge bank of interior windows reveal a massive, Willy Wonka-ish roasting facility at the center of which are vintage Probats from the 1930s and 1950s. (You'll have to do without the river of chocolate.)

ESPRESSO VIVACE

THE ICONIC, ENER-
GETIC PERSONALITY
BEHIND ESPRESSO
VIVACE IS
PERHAPS MORE
RESPONSIBLE THAN
ANY OTHER
INDIVIDUAL IN THE
U.S. FOR ELEVATING
ESPRESSO
TO HIGH ART.

ARTISTIC, PRECISE, MUSTACHIOED

David Schomer, founder of Espresso Vivace, is a wiry, mustachioed ball of pure energy barely contained in human skin. In 1988 he bought a coffee cart on a supposedly temporary detour from becoming a classical flautist. Espresso quickly became his art. The creative aspect of coffee drives him, but he also has a scientific side. Early in his life, Schomer was a measurement scientist for Boeing, where he learned the precision control of variables to achieve measurements accurate to the millionth part. By tinkering over the decades with grinders, espresso machines, water filtration, espresso tampers, and more, and publishing the results of his inquiries, he has significantly altered the coffee landscape across the U.S. Many of the most influential roasters profiled in this book discovered a love of coffee—and an inkling of its enormous potential as a culinary art—through Vivace in the 1990s.

ORIGIN OF THAT HEART IN YOUR CUP

If you've ever marveled at the beautiful heart or fern leaf (called a rosetta) a barista has added to the top of your latte using only a pitcher of milk, you can thank Schomer, who is well known for bringing latte art to America. Though Italians have long created such milky designs, the practice wasn't common in the U.S. until the mid-1990s when Schomer released a training video for baristas. He believes that latte art entices people to try new things—a coffee drink with less milk, for example. Another

BRIX ESPRESSO BAR:
532 BROADWAY AVE. E, SEATTLE

ROASTING SINCE '91

1000-5000 lb./week

on a Diedrich CR-30 roaster

FIND THE COFFEE AT ESPRESSOVIVACE.COM / THEIR CAFÉS

Latte art made its American debut at Espresso Vivace.

of his signature imports is the idea of grinding espresso beans immediately before pulling a shot to maximize flavor and crema. His experiments have also contributed significantly to the refinement of temperature control in espresso machines; thanks partly to him, water temperature doesn't fluctuate wildly, leading to unpredictable results. Schomer's many innovations have led to the continual refinement of the art of espresso.

THREE EXCEPTIONAL ESPRESSO BLENDS

The flagship café of Espresso Vivace is fittingly called Brix, a scientific term for the measurement of a liquid's sweetness. Schomer believes a roaster should have a point of view, and his is caramel. Vivace offers only three coffees, all of them espresso blends—Dolce, Vita, and decaf. Dolce is used for straight espresso shots, which are ordered with uncommon frequency by patrons in out-the-door lines at Seattle-area Vivace cafés. It is more lightly roasted and delicate, representative of the northern Italian style that Schomer fell in love with in Trieste. The Vita is similar to the Dolce, but its caramel is thundering. It's used in drinks with milk, like cappuccinos and lattes. The unique flavor of Vivace's espresso comes from an unusual combination of beans that includes Indian coffees. Vivace doesn't move with trends. It has done one thing since 1991— espresso—and done it to perfection, inspiring fierce loyalty. But Schomer also believes that a younger generation of coffee fiends with a different focus, like single-origin coffees of special provenance, are pursuing the same broad goal: improving coffee quality and the quality of life for coffee farmers.

HERKIMER COFFEE

ROASTERY AND ORIGINAL CAFÉ: 7320 Greenwood Ave. N, Seattle	ROASTING SINCE '07
SECOND CAFÉ: 5611 University Way NE, Seattle	

1000-5000 lb./week — on a Probat L25 roaster

FIND THE COFFEE AT HERKIMERCOFFEE.COM / THEIR CAFÉS

WHERE VINTAGE MEETS MODERN

Herkimer's logo is a riff on an old railroad bridge in Herkimer, New York, where owner Mike Prins's father grew up. The bridge is old; the logo, like the company, is artful and new. Walk into the original café and you'll notice vintage touches, like bolted-down bar stools, in a space that's otherwise clean and modern. Turn to the right and you realize the glassless windows you see—like those of an old railway observation car—peer onto a gorgeous roastery, which is dominated by a vintage Probat L25 but surrounded by every modern accoutrement. The space reflects decades of experience in coffee—Prins was a founder of Seattle's Caffé Vita.

COFFEE GEEK EXTRAORDINAIRE

It feels like magic, but it must be science. Head roaster Scott Richard-

> AT HERKIMER, COFFEE IS A BUSINESS BUILT ON PASSION. "YOU DON'T GET RICH DOING IT LIKE THIS, BUT IT DOES ENRICH YOUR LIFE."

son has just offered me four different shots of the same espresso, and he predicted exactly how each would taste. Richardson is a major geek in the biz, an inveterate tinkerer. Just now, he's illustrating pressure profiling, the idea that different amounts of pressure forced through espresso grounds will deeply affect flavor. Want a sweeter shot with a less grainy texture? Give the grounds a light blast of low-pressure water for a few seconds, then a few more of midline pressure, and then full bore at nine bars for the rest of the twenty-five-second extraction. Richardson has worked with an espresso machine manufacturer to build in better pressure control on professional equipment. It's just one example of his boundless nerdism. "I geek off on this stuff all day," he says.

A LITTLE EVERYDAY FLAWLESSNESS

In all things, Herkimer chases perfection. Their espresso blend (called, simply enough, Espresso Blend) unfolds in your mouth: enough acidity to open your taste buds and make your mouth water, followed by a sweet infusion of cardamom, clove, dark chocolate, and black cherry, the texture of champagne mousse. It's not easy to achieve this kind of precision when the ingredients are constantly in flux, coffees coming in and out of season. Coffees for the blend are like puzzle pieces that need to fit together—one for sweetness, one for acidity, and so on. Richardson relishes the challenge and enjoys working with Herkimer's baristas to deliver the perfect shot.

KUMA COFFEE

ONE-MAN SHOW

From buying and roasting the coffee, to stamping and filling the bags, Mark Barany does pretty much everything for his small coffee-roasting company himself. So perhaps it's not surprising that his list of Facebook friends includes nearly a hundred coffee growers. When he wants to find out more about a farm, he googles them. In the wake of pioneering efforts by companies like Stumptown to connect roasters and growers, littler roasters like Kuma are jumping into the fray, and technology is making it possible. Until 2010 Kuma was a hobby business, and Barany worked full time in the IT department at Seattle Pacific University. Now he's lucky (or crazy) enough to take on managing every aspect of Kuma on his own.

> KUMA'S MARK BARANY AIMS TO STEER SEATTLE'S TASTES IN A NEW DIRECTION.

PENCHANT FOR BRIGHT, FRUITY COFFEES

Kuma focuses on single-origin coffees and lighter roasts. The seasonal offering of Panama Elida, for example, has the creamy texture and blackberry fruitiness of yogurt. It's one of Barany's favorites, though many of his Seattle customers haven't quite come around to a preference for the fruity, floral coffees he loves. Kuma's signature Red Bear espresso blend is more toned down, with only a kiss of brightness. You can enjoy it—or one of Barany's prized single origins—at a low-key coffee bar at the edge of the Fremont neighborhood.

TRANSPARENT PAYMENTS TO FARMERS

In 2010 Barany became one of the first West Coast coffee roasters to publish on his website the prices he pays to farmers and importers for green coffee. In 2011 he paid between $2.80 and $3.50 for green coffee, the latter for the exceptional Panama Elida. Though coffee roasters like to throw around the word transparency, few provide concrete numbers even at this modest level.

CAFÉ:
4147 STONE WAY AVE. N, SEATTLE

ROASTING SINCE

'07

Less than 1000 lb./week

on a Probat L12 roaster

FIND THE COFFEE AT KUMACOFFEE.COM / THEIR CAFÉ

LIGHTHOUSE ROASTERS

FROM A HIGH HILL IN THE FREMONT NEIGHBORHOOD, LIGHTHOUSE ROASTERS HAS BEEN A SUBTLE BEACON FOR SEATTLE COFFEE LOVERS SINCE THE EARLY 1990S.

A DEDICATED, NEIGHBORLY FOLLOWING

Lighthouse Coffee Roasters sits at the apex of a sleepy neighborhood street, surrounded by tidy houses like boats in a harbor. A vintage German Gothot roasting machine churns away at the back of the store, just like it would have in an early twentieth-century five-and-dime. (The nearly century-old building was originally a grocery store.) Meanwhile, devoted locals read the paper and talk to neighbors over steaming lattes. Laptops are noticeably absent from the scattered tables. It could be the most neighborly café on the West Coast, the kind of place where you could walk up to the man pouring a 150-pound burlap bag of coffee beans into a roasting machine and begin chatting. That's owner Ed Leebrick, by the way, and he's been roasting coffee here since 1994.

SHARING ROASTING KNOW-HOW

Despite its humble living-room demeanor, Lighthouse has had an outsized impact on American coffee culture, though few would know it. Leebrick learned to roast from Northwest coffee dynamo Tim McCormack, one of the original Starbucks roasters. According to stereotype, roasters are secretive about their craft, but Leebrick has been generous with his knowledge, helping independent roasters nationwide learn to roast and source specialty coffees from small farms around the world. Duane Sorenson, for one, trained at Leebrick's feet in the 1990s before going on to develop his own ideas about coffee roasting and opening Stumptown Coffee Roasters in Portland.

ENDURING, WELL-DEVELOPED COFFEES

Lighthouse's Espresso Blend is deeply sweet and tinged with bitterness on its own, but sits comfortably in a latte. The toothsome signature drip blend, Roaster's Choice, is much beloved by regulars. On the café's unpretentious chalk-drawn menu, you'll also find a list of single-origin coffees (Lighthouse calls them varietals and identifies them only by country).

Leebrick isn't concerned about things like labeling the elevation at which each coffee is grown. When he opened the café and roastery in the early 1990s, he bucked the trend of extreme dark roasting popularized by Peet's and Starbucks. Now that the pendulum of taste has swung in the other direction, Leebrick continues to roast well-developed coffees that suit his loyal customers just fine. Like the landmark lighthouses that dot the West Coast, Lighthouse has an aura of immovability.

ROASTERY AND ORIGINAL CAFÉ:
400 N 43RD ST., SEATTLE

ROASTING SINCE

'94

1000-5000 lb./week

on a 23-kilo Gothot roaster

FIND THE COFFEE AT LIGHTHOUSECOFFEE ROASTERS.COM / THEIR CAFÉ

SEATTLE COFFEE WORKS

SCHOOLED BY A PLUMBER'S PALATE

The don of SCW is Sebastian Simsch, a coffee fanatic with a Ph.D. in history. To get through writing his dissertation, he bought himself a home espresso machine. One afternoon he offered to make a shot for a plumber working on his house. In true Seattle fashion, the plumber had a better palate than the doctoral student, and Simsch realized his espresso was horrible. The plumber took him to legendary Hines Public Market Coffee (now closed), where he had his first "divine" espresso. Simsch quickly abandoned history for coffee. In 2006 he opened SCW across the street from its current location.

DIRECT TRADE FOR QUALITY CONTROL

During its first three years, SCW was the only Seattle café featuring espres-

JUST STEPS FROM PIKE PLACE MARKET IS SEATTLE'S ONLY DOWNTOWN ROASTERY-CAFÉ, A BRIGHT, BUSTLING FORCE ON THE CITY'S COFFEE SCENE.

so from different roasters side by side. It gave Simsch a rare opportunity to hone his palate and his barista skills on a rotating crop of top-notch coffees. Knowledge gained, Simsch converted SCW to a microroastery and began to roast his own. He believes strongly in showcasing the single-origin coffees he purchases directly from farmers, even though most of his coffees are mixed into blends for drip and espresso. He believes direct trade fosters a relationship allowing both the farmer and roaster to influence quality—less a marketing gimmick than a business model.

PREMIUM COFFEE FROM SMALL FARMS

You can appreciate one of SCW's high-quality, directly traded coffees at the downtown café's slow-coffee bar, one of few in Seattle. At a secluded counter adjacent to the main bar, you can pull up a stool and watch as a barista prepares a coffee of your choice using whatever method you prefer: Chemex or Hario pour-over, vacuum pot, or individual French press. It's the perfect place to try a cup of Guatemala Antigua Finca Aurelio y Lorena, which has the sweet, thick flavor of marshmallows. The small farm where it originates, operated by the eponymous Aurelio and Lorena, produces only three bags of coffee a year, and all of it goes to SCW. It is only available in summer.

ROASTERY AND CAFÉ:
107 PIKE ST., SEATTLE

ROASTING SINCE
'07

1000-5000 lb./week

on a Diedrich IR 12 roaster

FIND THE COFFEE AT SEATTLECOFFEEWORKS.COM / THEIR CAFÉ

SEATTLE'S BEST COFFEE

TIRELESS ADVOCATE FOR QUALITY

325 CAFÉS NATIONWIDE

ROASTING SINCE '70

More than 100,000 lb./week

FIND THE COFFEE AT SEATTLESBEST.COM / THEIR CAFÉS

In 1971, Jim Stewart opened the Wet Whisker coffee and ice cream store on Seattle's Pier 70, after relocating from Whidbey Island. It was the same year that Jerry Baldwin, Gordon Bowker, and Zev Siegl started selling beans in a Pike Place storefront called Starbucks. Within a few years the Wet Whisker would morph into Stewart Brothers Coffee, and then, in 1991, into Seattle's Best. What never changed was Stewart's pioneering commitment to sourcing coffees. Before the coffee-roaster-as-intrepid-world-traveler stereotype had emerged, he was journeying across the globe to visit coffee fincas and work with farmers. Stewart also worked tirelessly to educate customers about the inherent characteristics of different beans, encouraging drip brewing and other simple ways to showcase a coffee's complex flavors. No longer connected to Seattle's Best, Stewart now owns Finca El Gato, a coffee farm in Costa Rica.

CURIOUS OPTIMISTS, TRY LEVEL TWO

Though Seattle's Best was once a small company, by the time Starbucks acquired it in 2003 it had experienced a decade of growth and expansion. The original roasting facility on Vashon Island was closed (it's now The Vashon Island Coffee Roasterie), and operations were folded into Starbucks' plants. But Starbucks retained the Seattle's Best brand identity, targeting an audience more interested in drip coffee than espresso with milk and syrups. A massive rebranding campaign in 2010 led to Seattle's Best renaming its coffees according to so-called levels, each oddly correlated to a personality type. (If you're a "curious optimist" you might enjoy level two, which has "low body" and a "lively acidity." Leaders "in both work and play" might prefer level five, the darkest roast.) The old

NOW A MAJOR SUBSIDIARY OF STARBUCKS, SEATTLE'S BEST WAS A COFFEE ORIGINAL WHEN IT STARTED IN THE 1970S.

signature blend Henry's (named after Stewart's cat) is now roughly equivalent to level four.

MORE THAN FIFTY THOUSAND LOCATIONS

Though Seattle's Best was once a resolutely Northwest company, these days you shouldn't have trouble finding the brand anywhere in the U.S. With a new logo, the company made a massive push to increase the number of locations where the coffee is sold. By signing agreements with movie theaters, the Burger King chain, and cruise lines, and by drastically increasing franchises, Seattle's Best can now be found in more than fifty thousand places (up from three thousand in 2009).

STARBUCKS COFFEE COMPANY

ORIGINAL CAFÉ:
1912 PIKE PL.,
SEATTLE

ROASTING SINCE

'71

More than 100,000 lb./week

FIND THE COFFEE AT STARBUCKS.COM / THEIR APPROXIMATELY 17,000 CAFÉS WORLDWIDE

THE FRANCHISE THAT STARTED IT ALL

A straight shot of espresso from Starbucks may be among the worst-tasting substances on Earth, but even the most inveterate coffee snob will own up to the fact that without Starbucks, none of it would be possible. Not only did the megaroaster introduce specialty coffee to the masses, it also accustomed us to paying more for higher quality. It's an old saw that Starbucks is really in the business of selling milk. But without the $4 latte, there would be no $8 Panama Esmeralda Especial. Starbucks also introduced the coffee shop as the quintessential third space—neither home nor work but another part of the fabric of community life. For that, every independent coffee shop in America owes its success to Starbucks.

LOVE THE COMPANY OR HATE IT, STARBUCKS IS INDISPUTABLY RESPONSIBLE FOR MODERN AMERICAN COFFEE CULTURE.

PATH TO WORLD DOMINATION

Starbucks wasn't always a behemoth. The company's founders, Jerry Baldwin, Gordon Bowker, and Zev Siegl, built the first store by hand for less than $10,000. It was just a few blocks away from the current "original" store in Pike Place Market, where baristas ham it up for tourists and pull shots on a nonautomated La Marzocco four-group espresso machine. The original Starbucks sold only whole-bean coffee and coffee makers—no espresso machines, no grande triple half-caf caramel lattes. Howard Schultz came on as marketing director in 1982 and eventually convinced the owners to serve Italian-style drinks. It was the beginning of Starbucks as we know it. Schultz bought the company from Baldwin and Bowker in 1987,

and so began the company's rapid expansion. Within a decade Starbucks had outposts across the globe. They now operate in fifty-five countries and in 2010 purchased 269 million pounds of green coffee.

FREQUENTLY DERIDED DARK ROAST

Many roasters openly speak of "Charbucks," a reference to the idea that Starbucks overroasts in order to hide the real flavors of lower-quality beans, but the company has never copped to that accusation. Certainly, Starbucks raised the bar in the late 1970s and early 1980s when most widely available coffee was instant. Because the company has either successfully pushed or successfully capitulated to consumer demand for ever-larger sizes with lots of sugary syrups, their coffee has to hit a certain flavor note hard to cut through the added ingredients. For better or worse, they achieve this by roasting dark.

CLASH OF THE MARKETING STRATEGIES

In part to combat criticism and years of declining sales, Starbucks has focused increasing attention on corporate social responsibility. They invest heavily in coffee-producing countries (including newcomers like China) through farmer loan programs and infrastructure creation. Though these are highly marketable maneuvers, the company does appear to have charted a direction for the future, with a goal of reducing energy consumption and waste, and purchasing most of its coffee under social responsibility and transparency standards (in 2010 more than 10 percent of the coffee they purchased was Fair Trade or organic

certified, but far more meets the company's own sustainability standard, called CAFE). At the same time, Starbucks aims to get more of its coffee into homes with a line of instant VIA brand coffee, Keurig-style prepackaged single-cup servings, and more bottled noncoffee beverages. Flagship cafés in Seattle (including one near Pike Place and another on Olive Way) and other cities have been rebuilt to LEED standards with exposed beams made of reclaimed wood, lots of natural light, and sleek, low-profile bars that allow you to see the baristas working. Baristas have been retrained and total automation scaled back. In short, Starbucks is trying to revivify the brand with tastemakers, while simultaneously targeting less frou-frou consumers at home.

VICTROLA COFFEE ROASTERS

GREEN THUMBS AND A LOVING APPROACH

The most prized coffee at Victrola doesn't have to cross half the world on a ship as other coffee does. It grows, a mere handful of cherries each year, in Seattle's Capitol Hill neighborhood. The beans come from a single potted coffee plant, about 10 feet tall, that lives in a light-filled training lab at the back of the Victrola roastery (weekly public cuppings are held in the same room). With a lot of loving care, it took three years to bear its first crop, enough for a single cup of coffee. That dedicated caretaking is typical of Victrola's approach to every aspect of roasting and serving coffee in their three comfortable Seattle cafés.

EXCEPTIONAL SINGLE ORIGINS

Victrola is one of the few places in Seattle serving single-origin espresso

> VICTROLA IS SEATTLE'S BEST-KNOWN QUALITY-FOCUSED THIRD-WAVE COFFEE COMPANY.

and offering brewed coffee prepared to order different ways (such as in a vacuum pot, pour-over, or French press). At any given time they may offer five to seven unique single-origin coffees, all purchased for being "classic" representations of a particular coffee-growing region or for their novel flavor. An example of the latter is Ethiopia Nekisse, a coffee exploding with silky berry flavors that come from meticulous natural processing. Victrola's customers have come to

Victrola's well-loved
coffee shrub.

expect these special coffees and are willing to pay more for them ($40 per pound for the Nekisse).

DIFFERENT OWNER, SAME VISION

Seattle's coffee cognoscenti were nervous in 2007 when word spread that Victrola's founders, Jen Strongin and Chris Sharp, were selling the company. The news that Dan Ollis was the buyer wasn't immediately reassuring—he owns the decidedly mainstream Whidbey Coffee, whose main locations include drive-throughs, hospitals, and a mall. But he kept true to the Victrola vision. Ollis quips that he knew one thing immediately: if he had tried to bring flavored iced granitas onto the menu, Victrola's baristas would have taken him out back and—well, they probably just would have quit. Instead, he's helped the young, passionate company get organized. All three Victrola locations are neighborhood fixtures, hosting community events, art installations, and live music, while gently nudging Seattleites to drink a better cup of coffee.

ROASTERY AND FLAGSHIP CAFÉ: 310 E PIKE ST., SEATTLE

ROASTING SINCE

'03

1000–5000 lb./week

on a Diedrich IR-12 roaster

FIND THE COFFEE AT VICTROLACOFFEE.COM / THEIR CAFÉS

ZOKA COFFEE ROASTERS AND TEA COMPANY

GROWING BUT STILL DOWN-TO-EARTH

At the University of Washington in the 1970s, Jeff Babcock drank Alfred Peet's coffee and fell in love. After trying to run a roasting company in his native Florida (a predictably painful experience), he headed back to the Northwest. Teaming up with Tim McCormack, one of the original Starbucks roasters, Babcock opened the first Zoka café in 1996. A little roasting machine sat right in the store. Now, with nearly fifty employees, multiple cafés in Seattle, a partner roastery in Japan, and an expanding business in grocery stores across the Northwest, Zoka is undoubtedly growing. But Babcock considers it a true-grit sort of growth, the kind that allows the company to offer health insurance to its employees and plan twenty years into the future.

TAKING BARISTAS SERIOUSLY

A poorly trained barista can botch the best coffee in the world if they don't know what they're doing. On a visit to Norway years ago, Babcock was stunned by the quality and professionalism of the baristas he met. The experience led him to institute a certification process for his employees at Zoka, an uncommon undertaking among American roasters. Every barista receives four hours of training a month to help ensure patrons never end up with a sour, underextracted espresso shot or scalded milk. As you

> ZOKA ELEVATES THE ART OF BEING A BARISTA.

might expect, Zoka's coffee slingers do well in barista competitions. In fact Babcock helped create the barista championship movement, which pushes the public to view baristas as serious professionals. Many ex-Zoka baristas have gone on to lifelong careers at prestigious coffee companies around the U.S. In addition to well-prepared coffee, you'll find a lot of smiles at Zoka's handful of large neighborhood cafés, where ample seating and free Wi-Fi encourage folks to settle in for a few hours at a time. (A smaller café is located downtown.)

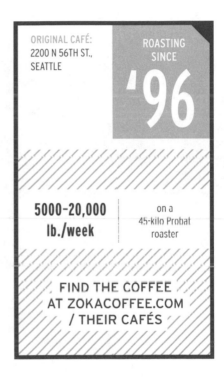

ORIGINAL CAFÉ:
2200 N 56TH ST., SEATTLE

ROASTING SINCE

'96

5000–20,000 lb./week

on a 45-kilo Probat roaster

FIND THE COFFEE AT ZOKACOFFEE.COM / THEIR CAFÉS

ESPRESSO THAT GOES BIG

Zoka's signature espresso blend, Paladino, is roasted for "symphonic effect." Like all espresso, Paladino has big flavor, but there's nothing surprising in it. That's the point, says Babcock, who adds that Seattle's coffee tastes are decidedly middle-of-the-road. In addition to Paladino and a half-dozen other blends, Zoka carries four or five single-origin coffees at any given time. Babcock stumbles upon these special coffees when visiting farms to negotiate the purchase of shipping containers (37,500 pounds) of coffee used in the blends. At the Kirkland location (129 Central Way) a single-origin espresso bar showcases recent, seasonal coffees.

VELTON'S COFFEE ROASTING COMPANY

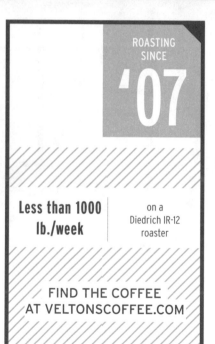

ROASTING SINCE

'07

Less than 1000 lb./week | on a Diedrich IR-12 roaster

FIND THE COFFEE AT VELTONSCOFFEE.COM

WELL KNOWN AMONG DEVOTEES

Velton Ross roasts only a few hundred pounds of beans a week and has no café of his own, yet his miniscule company enjoys a national reputation thanks to its connection to the vast network of coffee zealots known as home baristas. The most dedicated among them wouldn't blink an eye at dropping $400 for a coffee grinder or $2000 for a single-group La Cimbali espresso machine that has to be hard-plumbed into their home's water line. Seattlecoffeegear.com, a major source for home espresso equipment, also sells Velton's coffees, and many home baristas are introduced to the roaster through the site.

ESPRESSO BLEND EARNS HIGH MARKS

Velton's medium-roasted Bonsai Blend earned 94 out of 100 points from coffeereview.com, one of the highest scores ever for an espresso blend. Its main component is a naturally processed Mexican coffee that, when fresh, tastes like a big gulp of strawberry-chocolate milk. Ross adds Sumatran (20 percent) for body, Brazilian (20 percent) for nuttiness and to mellow the Mexican, and Ethiopian or Central American (10 percent) for crisp, citric brightness. The end result is smooth and pointedly sweet, a stellar espresso blend. The Bonsai is pudding-proof that having a standout signature blend is a good way for a roaster to distinguish his coffees.

REGIONALLY UNIQUE SINGLE ORIGINS

Specializing in estate single origins, Ross seeks out great balance, a clean cup, and distinct acidity.

For him, a great coffee won't have just one flavor; he looks for four or five adjectives to describe how the taste evolves in your mouth. He also goes out of his way to use importers other than the usual suspects, so many of his single-origin coffees are unique among Northwest roasters. Ross roasts many of his single origins longer and more slowly than other microroasters might, to a medium shade, so that they can be used as espresso, in part because of his espresso-addicted home barista followers.

THIS TINY ROASTER HAS MADE INROADS WITH COFFEE'S BIGGEST FANATICS: HOME BARISTAS.

BELLINGHAM

MANIAC ROASTING

THERE ARE TWO KINDS OF COFFEE ROASTERS: THOSE WHO HAVE SET THEIR MACHINES ON FIRE, AND EVERYONE ELSE.

FIERY LAUNCH INTO ROASTING

After being kicked out of college in Greeley, Colorado, Alexarc Mastema roasted coffee at a Denver café. Part of his job was to answer customers' questions while he roasted. One day he lost track of the roast while chatting away and failed to notice the beans had caught fire. (He subsequently lost track of that job.) Luckily the experience didn't cure Mastema of his obsession with coffee. He eventually found his way to Bellingham, a liberal college town that serves as a jumping-off point for exploring the San Juan Islands. With a partner, $15,000, some home improvement manuals, and a lot of elbow grease, he built himself a café, naming it the Black Drop Coffee House.

TATTOOS, PIERCINGS, SINGLE ORIGINS

The countercultural atmosphere in Bellingham suits Mastema, who is even more heavily pierced and tattooed than your run-of-the-mill indie coffee roaster. (Fittingly, two black drops inked on his wrists commemorate his hard labor.) He accepts but gently challenges the general mania in Bellingham for certified coffees (organic and Fair Trade in particular) and old-school dark roasts at the expense of higher-quality or new and exciting coffees. Responding to demand, he offers The Darkness, usually a mix from Colombia, Mexico, and Guatemala. But Mastema takes extra care to offer more lightly roasted beans and the bright, snappy single-origin coffees he loves most.

THE CHARM OF UN-LIKELY CONNECTIONS

To scratch his itch for roasting, Mastema sold the Black Drop to his employees and now devotes all his energy to Maniac. The Black Drop remains Mastema's biggest client, however, and is certainly the best place to experience Maniac coffees.

The comfy, funky corner café remains deeply connected to the ethos of Mastema's approach, which is about linking people together—from the farmer to a carefully coiffed, pant-suited customer to Mastema himself, tattoos and all. It's the unlikeliness of some of those connections, inspired by something as small as a coffee bean, that keeps him roasting.

ROASTERY & STORE:
205 GRAND AVE.,
BELLINGHAM

BLACK DROP
COFFEE HOUSE:
300 W CHAMPION ST.,
BELLINGHAM

ROASTING SINCE

'07

Less than 1000 lb./week

on a Primo PRI-TTEC roaster

FIND THE COFFEE AT THEIR ROASTERY-STORE / BLACK DROP COFFEE HOUSE

ISLAND HOPPING

L et's face it: coffee is a convenient excuse for travel. The San Juans and the islands of Puget Sound are some of the most beautiful territory in the U.S. Life on the islands (and in the handful of mainland towns facing Puget Sound) is laid back, but being the maritime Northwest, it's also rainy as all get-out. That may explain why so many coffee roasters hide out there. Island roasters tend to have charming little shops with lots of personality. The quality isn't always stellar, but who cares—you're ferry-hopping, remember?

BELLINGHAM (MAINLAND)

Guadalupe's Coffee Roaster (guadalupescoffee.blogspot.com).
Available at the Bellingham Farmers' Market, April through September. Medium- and dark-roasted coffees that are sustainably grown and ethically traded.

Maniac Roasting (205 Grand Ave., maniacroasting.com).
Also available at the Black Drop Coffee House, 300 W Champion St. Light roasts, dark roasts, and bright single origins. (See also page 266.)

Onyx Coffee Bar (1015 Railroad Ave. #105, onyxcoffeebar.com).
Featuring coffee from multiple boutique roasters across the West Coast; owned by rock star coffee farmer Edwin Martinez of Finca Vista Hermosa in the Huehuetenango region of Guatemala.

SAN JUAN ISLAND

San Juan Roasting Company (18 Cannery Landing, Friday Harbor, rockisland.com/~sjcoffee). Sit back and enjoy the view from this quaint shop.

WHIDBEY ISLAND

Honeymoon Bay Coffee Roasters (1100 SW Bowmer Dr. Suite A-101, Oak Harbor, honeymoonbaycoffee.com). A small storefront is attached to the roastery so you can taste fresh-roasted beans anytime.

Mukilteo Coffee Roasters (3228 Lake Leo Way, Langley, mukilteocoffee.com). Coffee in a sylvan setting, with local art and occasional live music.

Useless Bay Coffee Company (121 Second St., Langley, uselessbaycoffee.com). One of the better cups of coffee available in Puget Sound. A small Probat roaster sits right in the café.

Whidbey Coffee (980 Pioneer Way, Oak Harbor, and other locations, whidbeycoffee.com). Owner Dan Ollis also owns Seattle's Victrola Coffee.

BAINBRIDGE ISLAND

Storyville Coffee Company (9459 Coppertop Loop NE, storyville.com). A mostly mail-order coffee company that offers only two choices: Prologue and Epilogue. Call ahead to drop in to the gorgeous, open-concept roastery for an informal tour.

VASHON ISLAND

The Vashon Island Coffee Roasterie (19529 Vashon Hwy SW, tvicr.com). On the site of the original Seattle's Best roastery, TVICR has a café and coffee museum onsite.

BATDORF & BRONSON COFFEE ROASTERS

DESPITE THEIR NATIONAL REACH, BATDORF & BRONSON'S HEART AND SOUL ARE IN THE NORTHWEST.

ENDURING TIES TO FARMS

Midway between Portland and Seattle, at the dead end of Olympia's Market Street, two things catch your attention: great piles of felled trees and the smell of roasting coffee. You don't get much more Northwest than that. Here sits the Port of Olympia, a timber hub and the national headquarters of Batdorf & Bronson. This is one of the bigger specialty roasters in the region, as a quick peek inside at dozens of huge piles of bagged coffee will confirm. Even so, they have been purchasing coffee directly from some of the same farms since the early 1990s. One such farm is La Minita in Costa Rica, which dries special lots of their beans in the sun at B&B's request.

EXPERT ROASTING IN SOARING SPACES

The roastery is the company's nerve center and performance space. This is where they roast their wildly popular Dancing Goats espresso blend, along with a tremendous array of single-origin offerings from Nicaragua to Indonesia. The building also houses a tasting room with giant windows connected to the sun-filled warehouse, giving visitors a chance to see the operation's guts. Their flagship café in downtown Olympia offers a similar expansiveness—ceiling joists soar overhead like a high railroad bridge, inviting in natural light that gives the space a warm air. There, too, an element of showmanship is on display, as baristas float from one end of the massive bar to the other, making coffee happen.

ROASTMASTERS AND BREW BATTLES

Batdorf & Bronson sees roasters as artisans. The roastmasters (three work out of both Olympia and Atlanta) are only allowed to spend half of their working hours roasting to preserve the focus they need to man the

machines. But roasting isn't the only thing B&B gets nerdy about. In 2010 they started hosting manual brew battles, wherein baristas compete to prepare the best cup of joe. No espresso, no latte art, no frills—just black coffee, mano a mano.

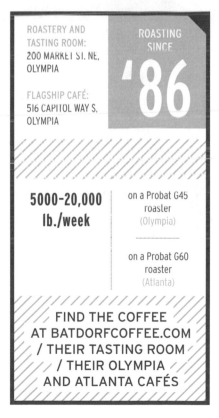

ROASTERY AND TASTING ROOM:
200 MARKET ST. NE, OLYMPIA

ROASTING SINCE '86

FLAGSHIP CAFÉ:
516 CAPITOL WAY S, OLYMPIA

5000-20,000 lb./week

on a Probat G45 roaster (Olympia)

on a Probat G60 roaster (Atlanta)

FIND THE COFFEE AT BATDORFCOFFEE.COM / THEIR TASTING ROOM / THEIR OLYMPIA AND ATLANTA CAFÉS

OLYMPIA COFFEE ROASTING COMPANY

OLYMPIA COFFEE
ROASTING
COMPANY IS AN
EXEMPLAR
OF THE
QUALITY-OBSESSED
SLOW-COFFEE
APPROACH.

QUALITY AND SUSTAINABILITY

As the capitol of Washington and home of ultra-liberal Evergreen State College, Olympia divides itself between button-down seat of government and funky college town. It has the right ingredients to be overrun with coffee snobs: a gray, water-logged winter and a highly educated populace in need of constant caffeine. Olympia Coffee Roasting opened in 2000 with a focus on certified organic and Fair Trade coffee, but overroasting produced dark, bitter beans. Happily, Oliver Stormshak steered the company in a new direction when he bought it in 2010. It is now strongly focused on single-origin coffees and meticulous sourcing, with a lighter roasting approach to highlight the special character of each bean. Stormshak believes in sourcing sustainable coffee but isn't rigid about certification—if he finds a superb coffee and witnesses sustainable growing practices on farm visits, he buys it, whether or not it's certified. Big Truck, the house espresso, is the only blend on offer.

SWEET AND CLEAN, PLEASE

According to Stormshak, three things define his approach: seasonality, quality, and "being boring." He doesn't like big, wild, or funky flavors. He's never carried an Indonesian coffee for this reason (wet hulling, a processing method used widely in Indonesia, imparts a flavor often likened to tobacco or marijuana). Stormshak prefers sweetness, cleanliness, and consistency. His favorite coffee,

ROASTERY AND ORIGINAL CAFÉ:
108 CHERRY ST., OLYMPIA

SECOND CAFÉ:
1706 HARRISON AVE., OLYMPIA

ROASTING SINCE
'00

1000-5000 lb./week

on a Diedrich IR-12 roaster

FIND THE COFFEE AT OLYMPIACOFFEE.COM / THEIR CAFÉS

Colombia Finca La Florida, which he buys directly from Manuel Antonio Ovies's small, 3-hectare farm, has a tealike clarity and on one tasting had the distinct flavor of sweet potatoes and cranberry sauce. The coffee is washed, allowing the flavor of the varietal (Caturra) and *terroir* to sing. It's remarkable.

UNIQUELY FOCUSED ON PROCESSING

Another Stormshak favorite comes from La Mirella in Costa Rica, the "healthiest-looking" farm he's visited, complete with "perfect soil, shade, and song birds." After their winter harvest, La Mirella processes the beans at their micromill in three different ways: washed, honey, and natural. Olympia Coffee Roasting pays for three extra laborers each year to assist with the natural processing, which requires additional work to keep the coffee from overfermenting inside the

coffee cherry in Costa Rica's humid weather. Stormshak wants his customers to understand the critical role that processing plays in determining flavor, so he carries all three versions of La Mirella's coffee in season. You can compare them side by side at one of Olympia Coffee Roasting's cafés.

SLOW COFFEE, ONE CUP AT A TIME

Stellar attention to detail is equally evident in the roastery-café. The coffee is always fresh: beans are pulled off the shelf seven days after roasting and donated to local nonprofits. At the main café—attached to the roastery, with a big window for peering in on the action—cups of regular coffee are prepared one at a time. Baristas use the slow-coffee approach to get customers thinking in a new way. They want you to know, for example, that this small Olympia café is the only place in the world you can drink

Manuel Antonio Ovies's coffee. The website plays a small but critical role in telling the stories of their coffees, providing rich, engaging background on the farmers. But Stormshak wishes he could do more: "I truly wish every one of my customers could meet every one of the farmers who grow the coffee they love."

CAFFÈ MELA

SURPRISINGLY GOOD COFFEE IN THE APPLE CAPITAL OF THE WORLD.

WHERE EVERYBODY KNOWS YOUR NAME

It's somewhat remarkable to find a big-city–style café in the middle of apple country (mela is Italian for "apple"), 140 miles from Seattle. Caffè Mela's flagship location, smack in the heart of downtown Wenatchee, is a friendly gathering place for the community. When locals stop by, they inevitably run into someone they know—like an episode of *Cheers* for the orchard set. Wenatchee folks have surprised owners Darren and Emily Reynolds with their willingness to transcend milky, flavored lattes and try something new, like one of the many single-origin or limited-edition coffees they feature. In 2010 Mela opened a drive-through location as well—*très* Wenatchee.

AN INTIMATE VENUE FOR LIVE MUSIC

Darren Reynolds wanted to be a musician until he concluded the lifestyle was rotten. He caught the coffee bug while working for an espresso parts company and decided to start a roastery of his own in a market less crowded than Seattle's. Since opening in 2005, Caffè Mela has made a big impact on local coffee and music culture. The main café has a 15-by-18-foot stage with a professional sound setup that Reynolds built. The Mela has become a stopover for top-notch musicians passing through town, who play for attentive (not to mention wide-awake) audiences in an intimate setting. Reynolds says he's heard more and better live music at the Mela than in all his years gigging in Seattle. Plus, the former musician gets to scratch his sonic itch.

LIGHTER ROASTS THAT EXPOSE ORIGIN FLAVOR

While working at the espresso parts company, Reynolds brewed a lot of coffee and got to try all the latest gadgets. The experience helped him understand what he prefers: light-medium roasts that let the coffee's origin flavor shine through (not unlike a beautiful guitar line cutting through the sound around it).

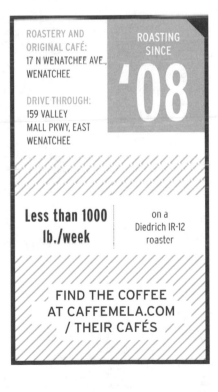

ROASTERY AND ORIGINAL CAFÉ:
17 N WENATCHEE AVE., WENATCHEE

DRIVE THROUGH:
159 VALLEY MALL PKWY, EAST WENATCHEE

ROASTING SINCE

'08

Less than 1000 lb./week

on a Diedrich IR-12 roaster

FIND THE COFFEE AT CAFFEMELA.COM / THEIR CAFÉS

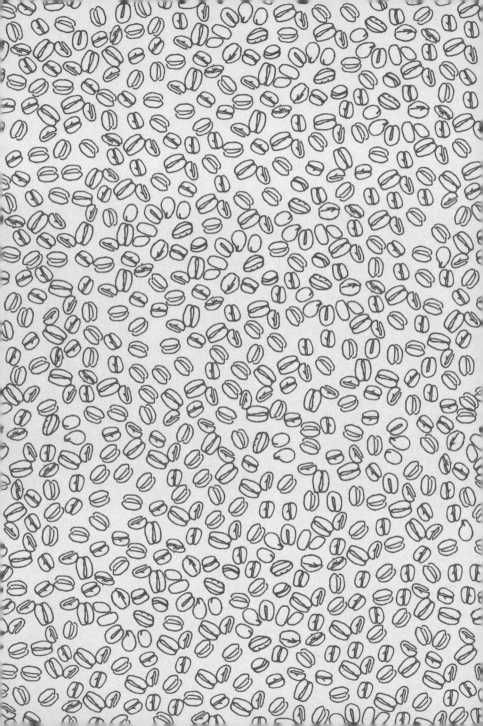

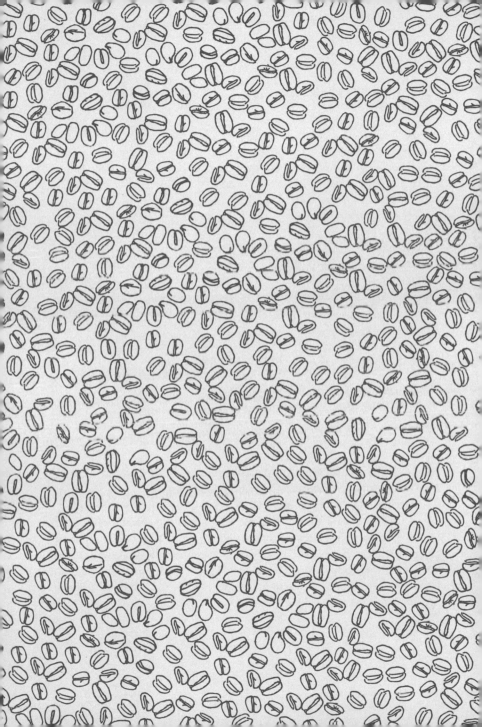

FURTHER READING

Somehow coffee tastes better when you know something about it. Whether you learn the name of the farm where it was grown, the name of the person who roasted it, or just a bit about the history of coffee, a little knowledge can make a good cup taste great.

Davids, Kenneth. 2001. *Coffee: A Guide to Buying, Brewing, and Enjoying*. 5th ed. New York: St. Martin's Griffin.
A classic hands-on guide to deepening your enjoyment of coffee, with overviews of major growing regions, instructions on making coffee at home, and more.

Davids, Kenneth. 2003. *Home Coffee Roasting: Romance and Revival*. Rev. ed. New York: St. Martin's Griffin.
This definitive how-to guide is full of background information about coffee and lots of tips and tricks for various roasting methods, from stirring beans in a skillet to using professional-grade home-roasting machines.

Park, Scott F., and Michael W. Austin, eds. 2011. *Coffee Philosophy for Everyone: Grounds for Debate*. Malden, MA: Wiley-Blackwell.
A collection of essays investigating the philosophical questions raised by coffee, written by a wide range of scholars and coffee people, including Mark Pendergrast and Kenneth Davids. Topics range from the aesthetic and moral (what it means to appreciate coffee and why it is important to do so) to the cultural (the role of coffeehouse in the public sphere) and athletic (caffeine as a performance enhancer). An uneven collection, but a few essays are particularly valuable.

Pendergrast, Mark. 2010. *Uncommon Grounds: The History of Coffee and How It Transformed Our World*. Rev. ed. New York: Basic Books.
This who-daddy history of coffee in America delves into the global forces shaping the coffee trade, the role of advertising, and the world of Big Coffee.

Ukers, William H. 2006. *All About Coffee*. 2nd ed. Mansfield Center, CT: Martino.
First published in 1922, this 796-page tome summarizes every aspect of the coffee business understood at that time. It was written and published by the editor of the *Tea and Coffee Trade Journal*, who knew the industry backward and forward. It includes incredible photographs from turn-of-the-twentieth-century coffee farms and cafés, a laugh-inducing list of euphemisms for coffee ("the liquor to heal all kings"), and more information about the historical coffee trade than seems possible to collect in one place.

Weissman, Michaele. 2008. *God in a Cup: The Obsessive Quest for the Perfect Coffee*. Hoboken, NJ: J. Wiley.
Weissman follows three mavericks of the third-wave movement (Stumptown's Duane Sorenson, Intelligentsia's Geoff Watts, and Counter Culture's Peter Giuliano) on their adventures around the world. As the title implies, these gents are looking for a lot of meaning in their cup of coffee, and Weissman helps explain their passion.

Wendelboe, Tim. 2010. *Coffee with Tim Wendelboe*. Oslo: Schibsted Forlag.
Wendelboe, the 2004 World Barista Champion, is internationally recognized for roasting some of the world's best coffee in his eponymous microroastery. His book is chock full of gorgeous photos and information about coffee from seed to cup, as well as detailed instructions for different ways to make the best possible cup at home. A great primer that encompasses more modern information about coffee than any other book.

RESOURCES

No coffee lover is an island. From green beans for DIY roasting, to equipment for making a great cup at home, to the latest gossip, aficionados need resources at their disposal. Here are some of the best.

Green beans

The Internet is a great place to start, but most small, independent coffee roasters are happy to sell loyal customers a few pounds of unroasted coffee. I've also seen numerous Ethiopian restaurants selling green coffee in Portland, and our fair city has its own green coffee retail store, Mr. Green Beans. Getting green coffee in person allows you to ask questions about it, and it's a neighborly way to go. If you're going to buy coffee online, begin with sweetmarias.com, the most informative, quality-focused site for home roasters (their buyers regularly collaborate with prominent West Coast roasters like Stumptown and Four Barrel).

Equipment

Coffee, like beer brewing or cycling, attracts a lot of gearheads. If you're one of them, the Internet is a great place to start building your collection of brewers, timers, scales, and spoons. (It's worth noting, however, that many independent roasteries and cafés also sell high-quality equipment for making coffee at home and will happily answer your questions and provide guidance.) Two essential online suppliers:

CLIVECOFFEE.COM

A carefully curated collection of coffee-brewing equipment, with an emphasis on elegant, sleek designs. They have a showroom in Portland. (See also page 176.)

SEATTLECOFFEEGEAR.COM

The big box store of online coffee equipment retailers. You can find pretty much anything here, from mini Japanese cold brewers to refurbished espresso machines from twenty different manufacturers.

Websites

Many websites are dedicated to coffee, and it seems like most roasters (and many baristas and home baristas) maintain blogs. There are too many sites to catalog here, but the following are a few of my favorites.

COFFEED.COM

Bills itself as a site for professionals and fanatics, and that's pretty much on the money. The discussion forum is mostly populated by baristas, roasters, and other professionals. Dropping in on their conversations can be fun just so long as you don't mind it sometimes getting a little judgy.

COFFEEGEEK.COM

Probably the largest and best-organized community website about coffee, with hundreds of discussion threads running at any given time. With editorials by founder and head coffee geek Mark Prince, as well as consumer reviews of equipment and tips covering everything from how to buy an espresso machine to how to achieve perfect microfoam in steamed milk.

SPRUDGE.COM

The Perez Hilton of the coffee world, Sprudge reports on the major comings and goings of the third-wave coffee scene, and has all the best gossip.

COFFEEREVIEW.COM

Kenneth Davids is the man behind this site, the coffee world's equivalent of *Wine Spectator*. On it, he (along with a crew of helpers) rates coffees from roasters across the country on a 100-point scale. His evaluations aren't the last word about any given coffee's flavor or quality, but it's a great place to discover new roasters and get a sense of their approach.

SWEETMARIAS.COM

Tom Owen and Maria Troy's site is aimed at home coffee roasters but provides a wealth of accessible, opinionated information about coffee in general, especially about the countries and small farms where exceptional coffee is grown. They offer fantastic, carefully selected green coffees just for home roasters (with a detailed profile for each), maintain a library of resources about coffee and roasting, and give plenty of hands-on tips for how to roast and make coffee at home. An invaluable resource for every coffee lover, even those who don't roast at home.

INDEX

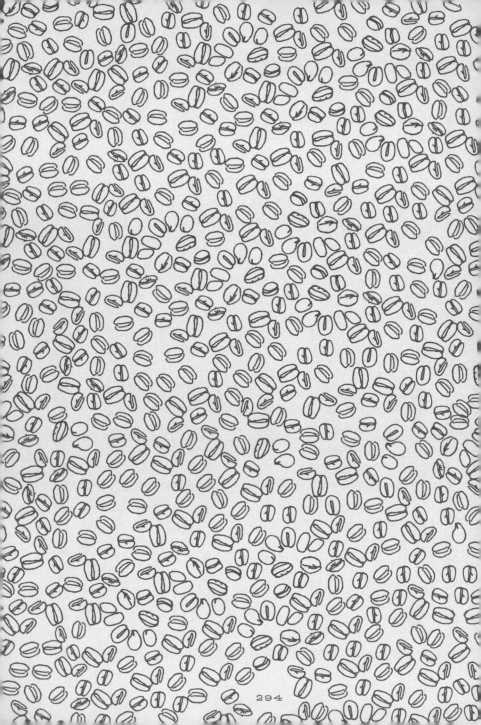

ABOUT THE AUTHOR

Hanna Neuschwander has written extensively about the quality-based coffee-roasting movement in the Pacific Northwest for publications including *Portland Monthly*, *Willamette Week*, and *Edible Portland*. She began her career in coffee working as a barista and has since judged regional barista competitions and written for *Barista Magazine*. She also writes about food and has produced several travel guides, including *Secret Portland* and *Secret Vancouver*.

Between the hours of nine and five, she is the communications director for the Graduate School of Education and Counseling at Lewis & Clark and the managing editor of *Democracy & Education*, an academic journal of progressive education theory.

Hanna lives in Portland, Oregon, with her husband, where they possess an entire kitchen cabinet full of devices for making coffee. She pollutes her morning cup with one sugar and a spoonful of cream, but takes all afternoon coffee neat.

photograph by Andy Pressman

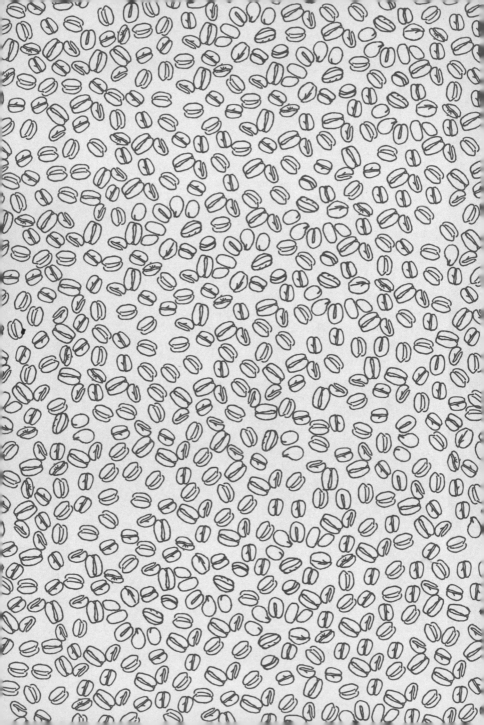